In the Twinkling of an Eye

A Book of Short Stories

SEYED MEHDI SHOJAEE

In the Twinkling of an Eye

A Book of Short Stories

Translated from the Persian
By Caroline Croskery

Printed by CreateSpace, An Amazon.com
Company
CreateSpace, Charleston, SC

U.S. Copyright © 2014 by Caroline Croskery, English Translator of Author Seyed Mehdi Shojaee's original work in Persian entitled "Bist Dastan" published by Neyestan Publishing, www.neyestanbook.com

Cover Design by Pejman Rahimizadeh

All rights reserved. This publication may not be reproduced, distributed or transmitted in any form or by any means including recording, photocopying or any other electronic or mechanical methods without the written consent of the copyright holder excepting brief quotations in critical reviews or as permitted by copyright law.

First Hardcover Edition, 2014.
Candle and Fog Publishing, Ltd.

Second Edition 2015
Printed by CreateSpace
eStore address:
https://www.CreateSpace.com/5304914
Available from Amazon.com and other retail outlets
Available on Kindle and other devices

ISBN 13: 978-1507893470
ISBN 10: 1507893477

Printed in the United States of America

Contents

Mahjabin 7
Stay! My Darling, Stay! 19
The Amateur Thief 29
Cain 1996 37
The Ring of Truth 43
The Wedding Shower 53
Santa Maria 79
The Last Defense 87
This Human Being… 101
Dead in the Water 121
Somebody Notice Me! 139
Signature 147
Anahita 155
I Need a Leili 167
The Pink Negligee 177
Breaking the News 185
The Spitting Image 195
Afsaneh 205
About the Author 211
About the Translator 213

In the Name of Love

Mahjabin

The dry desert looked to him like parched, cracked lips. As far as the eye could see there was nothing but footprints of thirst; patchy crevices and prickles that were sporadically emerging from the heart of the desert like a scruffy face rubbing against him.

The silence of the desert was occasionally disturbed by a mild breeze that blew heat and sand into his face. The man simply took off his shirt, brushed the sand off of his body and put the shirt back on again.

As he stroked his head, neck and chest, he found that sand kept sticking to him all over - and he noticed that his hands were still bruised. That morning when he was sneaking out of the village, a curious little boy studied him carefully and asked "Sir, Why are your hands and face bruised?"

He tried to cover his face with his hands to escape the grip of the boy's stare. "I don't know! Nevermind!"

The youngster kept following him, "But the bruise on your face is exactly like the one on Mahjabin's face!"

This remark alarmed him. He turned around and asked, "How do you know Mahjabin?"

"Who doesn't know her?"

"When did you meet her?"

"Just today; everyone has seen her."

Then in an instant the boy was gone. He felt his legs weaken and his knees give way underneath him as he sank to the ground.

Now where will you go, you disgraced one of the world?

When the sun came up, the people would surely take to the streets and alleys and form a circle around his house and crane their heads to catch a glimpse of this scandalous man. People would be gathering and making a scene on their rooftops and from over their garden walls.

One of the villagers shakes his head in disgust, saying in outrage, "This was our children's teacher!" Another says, "To what kind of person had we entrusted our girls?" A third one says, "From now on, we can't even trust our own eyes!"

And a fourth ...

He had to flee the village. An inner force had compelled him to abscond, but from whom was he escaping? From himself or from others? To where? He did not know. Perhaps there was some place where no eye would notice the bruise on his face and link it to the one on Mahjabin's face.

He looked back and saw the village that was now a dark spot in the distance and then turned and continued on his way. There was nowhere to go, either in his mind or in the desert. He put his hand into his shirt pocket and took out a white handkerchief which he unfolded with hesitation. He then cautiously opened the mirror and raised it up to his eyes and looked into it. It was a reddish-black bruise and looked like skin that had been burned with fire and was about to peel off. The wounds on his cheeks and lips were in exactly the same areas where he had touched Mahjabin.

"Sir, I have brought milk for you."

This was Mahjabin's daily work. She would come at sunrise and give three, gentle and successive taps at the door. The man felt the soft strokes of her delicate, outstretched hands and feminine fingertips caressing his heart. His door was always ajar.

Moments later, the old panel of the door would frame her heavenly image with her chestnut hair spilling onto her shoulders and her perfect, long eyelashes shading her dreamy brown eyes like a canopy. He always thought that her skin and face were like petals blooming from her rosebud lips.

At their first meeting, he imagined it was a dream or heavenly reverie only experienced by angels at daybreak. Then her eyelashes fluttered and she offered the bowl of milk, and her lips ... her lips parted as she said:

"I have brought your milk, sir."

It was only then when he realized the image in the door frame was not a dream or a mental representation. He didn't know what it was. He only knew that she would appear daily with soft, gentle steps, place the bowl of milk into his hands, retrieve the bowl from the previous day and quietly disappear. No matter how hard he racked his brains to remember where he had previously seen the girl, it was to no avail. There was no trace of her in his mind. But how could this be possible? He had brushed up on the list of students in his classes over the past years, the students who had listened to his words and met his eyes one by one. Wherefrom then had this Mahjabin come?

That evening he left home without so much as combing his hair or looking into the mirror, but he combed every passage, lane and square in the village looking for her. In a state of agitation, he brushed off all those who invited him into their homes for tea, flinging a nervous greeting in passing. He even stopped down by the river where the girls spent their time washing clothes.

A girl who had spread her blue-colored chador over a branch had told him, "Why have you left your home sir? If you needed anything, you could have asked us."

He replied, "I'm just out for a breath of fresh air." He hurried away, keeping on with his search and taking no notice of the approaching dusk. It was finally nightfall when one of the boys brought him a lantern and told him, "Sir you might fall without a lamp." Since he still had not found her, they insisted on accompanying him back to his home. He dared not ask anything of anyone but preferred to continue this blind search without revealing his secret to a soul.

He had completely put aside reading and writing in these few weeks. All of his thoughts and prayers were focused on Mahjabin, who would appear every morning and ignite a flame, which burnt within him before she went swiftly away.

Why had he not spoken to her in all that time? Why had he not inspired her to speak? Why had he not made her sit or even stand for just a few words? What a thought! Speaking in the presence of that statue of beauty, that icon of elegance was the most difficult thing to do, something equal to impossibility.

On these occasions, if it had been in his power, he should have poured all of his attention and appreciation for her majesty and beauty into his gaze not to let a portion of it leave his sight or its delicacy be lost.

He wrapped the mirror in the handkerchief again, slung his shirt over his head to serve as a shield against the direct heat of the sun and began walking towards that unknown destination. Thirst conquered his body moment by moment.

In all this time, he had never thought of kissing or touching Mahjabin. Even this morning before she arrived, the thought had never crossed his mind. Between the spark of impulse and action, there had been no time for reflection.

Mahjabin had held out the bowl to him. He took the bowl with his right hand and placed it on the shelf by the door. He touched her cheek with his left hand and then caressed her face with both hands. Her small lips parted with a blushing smile. A faint pink ran through her cheeks. He pressed his lips to her face and when he pulled back he discovered that her cheek was bruised exactly like his hands and lips.

Suddenly, he was overwhelmed by shame and embarrassment. He had not heard or read anywhere that the area one kisses would bruise. He looked at the palms of his own hands and fingers, and saw that the areas that had made contact with Mahjabin's cheek were now black and blue.

By the time he comprehended what he had done, Mahjabin had already dashed away. He looked into the mirror beside the door and saw that his cheeks and lips were also bruised. His head began to spin. His knees grew weak as he sank to the floor by the column near the door.

Bewilderment, astonishment and repentance resuscitated him like cold water. He wasn't thinking about himself; he was worried that Mahjabin's reputation would be tarnished moments later in the village.

He thought to himself that his face or hers alone would not indicate any crime or wrongdoing. Who would know how the moon-shaped blemish on his face had taken form or from where the cloud-like taint on Mahjabin's face had come? But if the two were seen side by side in one place, everyone in that village would know of their disgrace. He knew that for the sake of protecting her reputation, he must get up and leave immediately so that Mahjabin's honor would not be smeared.

Except for a small mirror, he took nothing with him, not even a bottle of water to prolong his life in the desert.

His tongue was dry and heavy like a lump of clay and the cracks in his lips were filling with blood. Even though he was not far from the village, he could no longer see it. The fire-like heat of the desert sucked the moisture out of his eyes and blurred his vision. He felt that his last breath of life was expiring. He slid to the ground as his eyelids closed.

The desert was his liver splayed beneath the sky; the sun's rays spearing it every moment. He thought his life was almost over, but couldn't imagine how he would navigate that step over the border of existence. His face was now flush with the desert. Out to his sides were his two arms, twitching on the ground like the two fins of a fish.

He slowly felt a damp, cold sense in the skin on his face. It was an invigorating moisture, injecting new life into his dying body. A pleasing shiver ran first through his face and then through his entire body, like a breath of life running through his lifeless form.

He propped himself up by his elbows and lifted his face off the ground. He thrust his limp hands into the damp sand and rubbed it all over his head, face and chest.

With each fist-full he dug, he discovered the sand beneath to be more damp and cold. It wasn't long before limpid water began to gush out of the ground. The distance between his hand and mouth seemed unbearable as he thrust his face into the pit and consigned his lips and mouth to the cold water.

    He felt like a new man as he got up - lively, cheerful and exhilarated. He suddenly remembered his hands. He raised them up to his eyes in trepidation, but did not see any trace of pigment. He frantically grabbed for his mirror, but couldn't find it anywhere. He raked the sand around him but found no trace of either the mirror or the handkerchief. Then his eyes unwittingly fell upon his image in the water that was more transparent than even a mirror, and he saw that no sign of the bruise remained.

    He wondered about Mahjabin. This bountiful spring should first have ... Mahjabin's face. He looked around. The village was closer than it had seemed before. He had to get her face to this water as soon as he could. He ran all the way to the village without any sense of fatigue. When he reached the threshold of the village, the old sorrow gripped his heart once more. Where could he find her now?

    Wasn't it true that he had never seen Mahjabin anywhere but in the doorway of his room? He must rush towards his house. There was greater hope of finding her there, though not at this time of morning rather at dawn. How was it possible to await twilight to come? With what had happened in the doorway this morning, how could he be sure that he would ever see her again? The young boy had said this morning that all people in the village knew Mahjabin, but had not Mahjabin been the name that *he* had given to this angel? He had never spoken to her or asked her name. How then could that boy know Mahjabin? How did the people of the village know her?

He asked the first person he encountered, "Do you know of a girl named Mahjabin?"

He heard, "No... Sir, you..." as he quickly passed the man. He didn't stop in case his demeanor might only increase the man's curiosity. The one thing *not* on his mind now, was reputation. He even asked the small boys in the alleys, "Do you ... a girl named Mahjabin?"

A young shoe-maker asked, "Sir, you who are always at home - where have you seen a girl like Mahjabin?"

An old shopkeeper said, "You know better dear teacher; we have no girl named Mahjabin in this village."

Up to the turn of the alley no one knew of a girl by the name of Mahjabin. When he passed the alley bend, he saw her shadow in his doorway. Amazed and astounded, he ran towards the house stumbling, losing his balance and twisting his ankle.

"You're here? This time of the day?"

"I have come to take back the bowl."

Amazed and astounded but docile and tame, he entered the house and returned with the bowl. When he handed the bowl to her, he remembered the mark on her face; the bruise which had now vanished.

He asked in amazement, "What happened to the mark on your face... that bruise?"

Mahjabin's lips and eyes moved with a unique calmness.

"Disappeared."

"How?"

"When you washed your face in the desert spring, around noon."

Mahjabin took out a folded handkerchief from the ruffle of her blue dress and handed it to him; it was a handkerchief he knew well. "Is this mirror also yours? You left it in the desert."

By the time he came around to framing his amazement in a question, Mahjabin had disappeared from the doorway. From the next day on, he perceived the vacant doorway only as a vague expectation.

Stay! My Darling, Stay!

Pressure! Intimidation! Impropriety!

Wherever you set foot, they first glare straight into your eyes, then look you up and down and shamelessly devise a way into your life.

They see you not as a human being but as a morsel walking upon the earth; a mere tool that existing for no other purpose than to provide the pleasure of others.

I placed the bottle of pills next to Javad's photo.

I said, "Javad, I can't go on like this. It may have been possible before, it isn't anymore. I can't take the pressure of this depressing life, these abnormal people with their brazen eyes and even more brazen hearts and rude mouths!

"Don't think because now that you are a martyr, you can shirk the responsibility of your wife and children!

"You've gone to the other side and are in heaven but you've left me with our two children to the mercy of God. When has God's justice ordered such a verdict? It's an outrage!

"Ok, fine. God knows that I have no one but Him and that I am not willing to lose Him at any cost. But I'm extremely troubled by God's creatures. I'm disgusted with them. I can't stand them.

"Last night I poured my heart out to God and said that I wished He had never introduced me to people as good as you, Javad. I wished that I had either not experienced those good times with you or these bad times without you!

"These are bad times, Javad. No one so much as gives another person a glass of water without self-interest being the motive. When I just now used the word 'water', I realized I forgot to bring a glass for myself so I could take all these pills."

I stood up. While I was talking to Javad I went to get some water. It crossed my mind that pills dissolve better in faucet water than in cold refrigerator water; and especially since all these pills need to dissolve quickly to get the job done.

"If you were in my place Javad, you would have done the same thing. Martyrdom is obviously easier than this abject life. Martyrdom is a desire to cut off from the material ... and then it is a joining. Well, I have felt cut off from everything for a very long time. The only thing left is joining you, and for that I am now making arrangements."

I emptied the bottle of pills into the glass of water and began stirring.

"The difference between what I am doing and martyrdom is that martyrdom requires an invitation, but I'm coming on my own. Martyrdom requires a kind of passport but I don't have one ... Javad! I know that what I'm doing is more like tearing up my identity card. It's as if I'm seeking asylum as an illegal refugee that doesn't even fathom what a passport or visa are .... And don't look at me like that, Javad. I know that suicide is the ugliest thing in the world, but uglier and more unbearable than that is going on living like this.

"You yourself witnessed this life. You saw what I had to put up with, not to mention all the foul language and evil treatment and the bad looks I had to endure.

"I wasn't tolerating everything for the purpose of accepting it all as normal, but only in the sense of avoiding confrontation with it. I forfeited my life and gave up everything that was considered normal and essential for a human being.

"When I come under question by even those closest to me just for rubbing a simple cream on my face to alleviate dry skin...they ask me why I'm doing that and for whom I'm doing it. It makes you want to forget the whole thing and just grin and bear it. That's what I mean - giving up and bearing it. Start with this small matter and go all the way up to the bigger issues handled by important people; those people who won't get the job done until they've collected on their bribe.

"They are the reasons a woman has to forfeit everything just to protect herself from the harassment; I finally gave up the permit I struggled so hard to get from the municipality, as well as the emergency loan action I had filed in court. I even forfeited my natural and normal rights.

"I tolerated this fate, quit my good job in the hospital and did whatever I needed to do to protect what I needed to protect. But now I feel I can't resist it anymore. I can't endure this situation anymore. I think that death is more honorable than this life.

"Your brother was here last night. He had come to call on me and his brother's children, our children. I asked him where he'd been all this time. I didn't ask him where he'd been all that time while you were fighting the war, Javad. I tried to maintain respect, and I did that because however a misfit he is, he is still part and parcel of you. When leaving, he brazenly looked into my eyes and said, 'If there is anything I can do or any *need* I can fulfill, give me a call.'

"I said abruptly, 'There is no *need*. Thank you.'

"He didn't leave. He stood there and went on to say, 'How is it possible for a young woman like you not to have any needs?' Javad, what would you have done if you were me?

"I also did the same. Damn! I violently slammed the door in his face, and then I wept until dawn.

"In the morning, I sent the kids to school sooner than usual. To answer their questioning looks told them that I needed to visit you. They thought I meant your grave.

"They began questioning me again to the effect that since we were used to going to your grave on Fridays together, why would I want to go now? Why all by myself?

"I said I felt miserable and would not find peace until I visited you.

"They calmed down, the poor babes, and then left for school. What plagued me was thinking about them coming home in the evening, turning the key in the lock, opening the door and seeing the lifeless body of their mother. It is a difficult thought, but more difficult than that is continuing this life."

The pills were completely dissolved making the water murky with white sediment at the bottom of the glass. I picked up the glass, guzzled it down, said my last prayer and laid my head down on the pillow, waiting for death to come.

I imagined that my head would first become heavy, my eyes dizzy and then I would fall into a deep sleep. I thought I would simply step from this side to the other side and finally reach peace. That is why I had chosen this method. I didn't want it to be ugly or messy, but I wanted it to be sure.

My head grew heavy, my eyes dizzy but I wasn't falling sleep. From under my droopy eyelids I could see Javad entering the room. I opened my eyes wide and gazed at him in disbelief. I was not at all astonished at the fact that Javad had left, but how he could have returned to our home?

I myself was going and naturally expected to see Javad. But I was still lying on the bed, the doors and walls, the window of the room, the glass, carafe of water and the crystal ice-cube holder on the table were all still in their place. Then I was still alive. I had not gone. I was in this world. My amazement was at how Javad had come to this side? How had he come? How had he opened the locked door?

I said, "Javad! How did you come to this side?"

He said, "You only perceive the existence of two sides from your perspective here on earth. But to us who look from above, it is all one."

"Have you come to take me?" I asked.

"No, I have come to keep you here."

"Javad!" I shouted, "Please don't joke with me like that. I'm not in the mood. I've cut myself off from the whole world. Don't make me cut off my hope in you as well."

He looked at me sternly, stood up and said, "I guess you no longer care in the slightest about my reputation."

I tried to grab hold of him but I could not. I said, "What does this have to do with your reputation? If that's the case, then every hardship I endured throughout all these years was because of your reputation. Is this my reward?"

He brought the empty container of ice from the corner of the room and sat down beside me and said, "My darling Shirin! Your decision today would have dishonored me before our children and family. All the years that I revelled and gloried in your strength and forbearance – if only I could show you the spot that has been reserved for you beside me in heaven. If only I could show you the superior rank you gained in the eyes of God on that night when you put our hungry children to sleep by telling them a bedtime story and you slept even more hungry than them - you surpassed even me on that night. If you could see the proportions of God's system, you would know that there are ranks and stations in heaven that cannot be achieved even by martyrdom, but can only be achieved by doing good and serving others."

"Javad! I've lost all hope."

He said, "If you open your eyes and your heart, you will feel hope again; there are as many paths to God as there are human beings on earth. And not just paths, but highways! But if you are looking to find hope merely in people, you may be disappointed."

I asked, "How much longer must I go on like this?"

He answered, "It'll all be over in the twinkling of an eye. If only it were possible to rise above this plane of existence and understand the fallacy of time. A whole lifetime is not even as long as a single day from an eternal perspective. Isn't it worth enduring this half day in exchange for lasting tranquility?"

I kept silent. He held the empty crystal ice holder in front of me and brought his hand close to my mouth. I opened my mouth and let him thrust his finger, that resembled a ray of light, down my throat. I brought up everything that was in my stomach.

I felt a lightness similar to the relief after giving birth. I smiled back at Javad's sweet smile and as I closed my eyes in exhaustion, I muttered, "You did it Javad! You made me stay!"

He quietly placed his two fingertips on my eyelids and caressed my cheeks, gently wiped my mouth and murmured softly, "Stay! My darling Shirin, stay!"

When I recovered, I saw that Javad had emptied the container, set the room in order and left just moments before – for the key ring was still swaying as it hung from the key in the door lock. Perhaps if he had shut the door more softly, I would not have woken up so soon.

The Amateur Thief

When from behind the window of the drugstore I first saw that person grappling with the lock of my car, I almost shouted, "Thief! Thief!"

But then I thought I had better to get over to the car, collar him and teach him a lesson myself. I stuffed the receipt into my pocket and darted out the door, running as fast as I could toward the car. I was just a few steps away from the car when I decided to get a hold of myself and keep calm so that I would be better able to catch the thief and hand him over to the authorities.

I slowed my steps and calmly walked over to him beside the car. I stood there without advancing any further as he was still looking around, struggling with the key.

I was now only one step away from him and could easily have jumped on him or grabbed him by the neck, tied his hands from behind or pummeled his side with my fists, or laid him out on the ground with a strong punch on the back of his head. But I preferred not to do any of these things.

I stood beside him and calmly, coolly asked, "Any problem? Can I help?"

Trying not to reveal his nervousness, he said, "No. It's just that I can't get my car door open."

He didn't look like a thief, even though you shouldn't be able to tell a thief by appearance. Yet his clumsiness and embarrassment indicated that he was at least not a professional. He looked and acted so pitiful that I had to ask, "Is there anything I can do to help you?"

While he was fiddling with the lock, he said, "No, thanks. I lost the key. I'm trying to get it open with a piece of wire."

I thought, "What nerve!" and I stood there staring at him.

I decided to carry out my plan and see where it would lead, because both the thief and the car were at hand and so there was nothing to worry about.

I said, "Do you want to try my key?"

He looked at me and said, "That's not a bad idea."

For my own confidence I added, "If it works, take me somewhere with you."

He took the keys and said, "Pray it works and I'll take you wherever you want."

When he inserted the key in the lock and the door opened, only then did he look at the other keys in my hand, "You probably have a car."

Unwittingly, I said, "Yes, I had one, but now I only have the keys."

Then I asked him, "What about you? Have you lost your the ignition key also or just the door key?"

"They were all together" he said.

I offered, "Let me try my car key. I've got the magic touch!"

He said ok and the car turned on with the very first start.

I said, "If you'll let me, I'll drive. It hasn't been that long since I've driven."

He paused for a moment and said, "I would prefer to drive myself."

I said, "As you wish."

I got out, walked around the car and climbed into the passenger seat. He was sitting in the driver's seat; for a moment I wondered what I would do if he drove away right then? But a strange peace fell over me as the thief opened the passenger door for me. I got into the car and he started driving. "Where do you want me to take you?" he asked.

"So you're keeping your promise?"

"Why not?" He was still nervous and looking around worriedly.

"You seem really restless. Are you feeling ok?" I asked him. We were now on the main street. He said, "I need to tell you something."

"Okay, tell me."

"Do you know why I didn't let you drive?" he asked.

"No, why?"

"I stole this car. I didn't want you to take the rap for it if we got caught."

My anger suddenly subsided. This thief seemed like a good guy.

"Why did you steal the car?" I asked him.

"Don't ask. I don't know why I told you this much."

I said, "I know why."

He asked in surprise, "You know?"

"Yes. It's because you're not a thief. You're inexperienced. It's your first time doing it."

He was distracted, ran through a red light and raised the voices of angry drivers.

"How could you tell?" he asked.

"It wasn't hard to figure out. You're too awkward to conceal your clumsiness."

He felt that the veil had been removed and he stood naked before me. His flabbergasted and disarmed look bore witness to this.

With a simplicity close to idiocy he asked, "Where do you want me to take you?"

"It doesn't matter. Just carry on wherever you're going. You can drop me somewhere on the way. But the answer to my question is important for me. Why did you steal the car?"

"I'm not a thief. I will also not remain a thief. I was forced to steal the car. And only this time!"

I asked, "What would you do if the owner saw you?"

"I would explain everything to him ..." Drops were rolling down his face as he fought hard to hold back his tears. "I would tell him that my child is in the hospital and I am helpless to provide for the expenses of his operation. I said I want to use this car to come up with as much money as I need for the medical expenses. Perhaps I'll sell only the tires. This sweet little girl shouldn't die because of the incompetency of her father!"

"Incompetency in stealing?" I asked.

He clammed up. I thought he had no answer.

Suddenly, he burst into tears, parked the car and answered through his crying, "To tell you the truth, yes. Incompetency in stealing. I was employed with a company as a manager of small department. I couldn't take all the upper management stealing. I had a fight with them and left the company."

Unwittingly, I blurted out, "From the frying pan into the fire. Stealing is stealing."

He got irritated to the point of shouting, "There sure is a difference. This is not the fire. The fire was over there at the company. That fire was hell. Here I'm only answerable to God for one person, not so many people."

"Why are you shouting at me?" I said, "It's not my fault."

He cooled down. Then he went on calmly but nervously and with a lump in his throat, "I'm sorry. When I was unemployed, I became depressed. I sold everything I had to keep up and now I don't know what to do. I can't help it."

"What would you do it the car belonged to you?" I asked him.

"I would work with it and earn a living as a taxi driver. I'm not above being a driver no matter how many years I studied at the university. What is important is that I would never go back to that old den of thieves."

I said, "Then work with this one. I also used to work with it. Don't remove the tires; that would be a pity. It is a beautiful car. Since the time I bought it, it has demanded nothing but water, oil and gas."

He was about to have a heart attack. He said, "You ... so ..."

"Nevermind," I said, "Here's the pink slip. Whenever you don't need it anymore, park it at the same place in front of the drugstore. I have a spare key. I will take it back then."

He said, "So ... you ..."

"Don't worry about me. My God is great. I've never reached a dead end yet."

The man's head dropped onto the steering wheel. I didn't want him to feel shame or start insisting that I not give him the car. So I got out of the car and quickly walked away from it.

***

A few nights later when a police officer appeared in front of our house with the pink slip, his first question was, "What was your relation to the man who suffered a heart attack a few nights ago at the steering wheel?"

I said in shock, "Relation? That man was me."

Cain 1996

We were walking on the top floor of the tallest building in the city. My brother said, "It's been decided," meaning that *he* had made the decision. "We'll give the tallest building of the city to the youngest child of the family. It will be both a place for him to work and rest, and a source for him to earn his livelihood as well."

While I was looking out at the beautiful vista of the city from the top of the building, I said, "I prefer to stand on my own two feet."

And with that comment, he calmly picked me up by the ankles and dangled me over the edge from that height which was the tallest building of the city.

However thin, tiny and scrawny I was, he was husky and stoutly built. I was like a child hanging in the air in the strong hands of a huge man.

My big brother knew that since my childhood I would get dizzy and nauseated at high altitudes. Maybe that's why he did that. It felt like my stomach was coming out of my mouth; I felt dizzy and tried not to struggle. After a few minutes when I started adjusting to being upside down, he pulled me up a bit so that my back was on the edge of the roof and my heels reached the roof.

I was still hanging in the air; what kept me dangling was him – holding me by my collar.
He said, "What do you do with a brother who won't do what you say?"

With a voice coming from the bottom of my throat I muttered, "Kill him maybe? It has always been that way since.."

He said, "I know about the story of Abel and Cain, you don't have to remind me."
I said, "I am ready."

He pulled me up a little and seated me on the edge of the roof. "You are wrong. We are not backward at least to the extent they were in those days."

I said, "Are you going to make it look like a suicide?"

He said, "I'm well aware of these methods."

I was about to catch my breath. I said, "You have become a master of these methods. You didn't used to be this skilled."

He said, "Conditions have changed."

He was right. After the death of father everything had changed; both conditions and people - but my brother more than all else.

Grandfather never needed to do or say anything. The gravity of his look was enough. Grandfather had the qualities of charisma and majesty about him while father had been gifted with grace and beauty. Those were the days when only a browbeating would render people submissive. Our quarrel started during grandfather's time.

I urged him, "Don't do that brother! Don't sell! Don't sell these manuscripts! Whatever we have is because of these manuscripts. Besides, grandfather would die of a broken heart if he knew that you were putting up our family's heritage for sale like this."

My brother has held a grudge against me ever since then. And from then on, whenever anyone ever spoke about the manuscripts, he would trace it back to me and it would strengthen his grudge against me even more.

He said, "You're a good kid. Your only problem is that you talk too much."

I said, "I am absolute silence. I don't say more than four words all day and night."
He said, "Don't fake idiocy. I mean the things you are writing."
I said, "Well, tell me what's wrong and I will correct it."
He said, "You're going too fast."
I said, "Of course, I'm not bad at the wheel. I keep my eyes peeled to the road..."
He interrupted me. "How I handle you isn't the criterion. I crash into those who cross me whether they like it or not; and the one who gets crushed in that accident is always the other party."
He was right. There were too many instances of nephews and nieces in our family ending up in the hospital, an insane asylum or a graveyard in an accident. Whenever an investigation was conducted, the findings would always be that they drove too fast.
I said, "Most of the children in our family ended up as addicts or gang members. Their lives were all ruined." He answered coldly, "Better than having them interfere in my affairs."
I said, "So, it's true that you put them in those situations?"
He said, "If they don't go along with me, I straighten them out. That's what I do."
My brother did construction work. He bought run-down properties cheap, fixed them

up with substandard materials and sold them at a profit.

Father would always shout, "Nothing good can come from this." But his warnings were always drowned out by the sound of shovels, picks and axes.

He sat me on the roof, let go of my shirt, glared at me furiously and said, "Get up and stand. I want to say two words." Suddenly, a strange fear overtook me.

You couldn't help it. We were all scared of my brother, some more, some less. It wasn't only because he was powerful and commanded all the family resources. There were many others who were more powerful than him but we weren't afraid of them. We feared my brother though, because we knew that he was dangerous and knew no bounds.

He himself didn't mind creating such feelings in people. Intimidation had always been an effective tool to dominate his brothers and dependents.

I was the only one left in the family who was not dependent on him. I struggled to survive by reciting poems, writing stories, doing paintings and making due with the least possible livelihood. But I was happy that I was standing on my own feet and was free to express my own words.

I stood up with difficulty. I didn't look into his eyes but kept my head lowered.

He said, "What vast properties do you own in this world that makes you so proud?"

I said, "I own nothing but my good reputation."

He said, "From now on don't count on it. One morning when you wake up you'll see it's all gone."

I said, "And how is that? I've done nothing wrong."

He scoffed and cleared his throat, and said with a feigned coolness, "If there's one thing I do well, it's extracting a false confession."

I felt a twinge of pain in my spinal column. Cold sweat trickled down my forehead. My knees felt weak as I sank to the ground.

The next morning when I read my own confessions I decided to report to the nearest legal authority. I was browbeaten.

The Ring of Truth

The doctor put his medical tools into his bag. He drew the white bedcover over Adam's face, turned to Hormat and said: "A stroke. It looks like he's been dead for a while."

Hormat was looking for a handkerchief to wipe her tears. She cried more with her nose than her eyes.

"Doctor, sir, when he came home last night, he was fine. He had dinner and took his cup of tea in his room - that is, here. In the morning I sent Roya to wake him up to buy milk. She knocked on his door but he didn't respond. No matter how many times I called to him from outside his locked door, no reply came. When I finally got in, I saw ..." and she burst out crying.

The doctor took out a stack of forms from his bag, "How old was he?"

Hormat was still crying, "32 years old."

"Were you on good terms with each other?"

"Why do you ask?"

"Well why were you living separate lives?"

Hormat no longer cried. "We were living in peace, each to his own. He couldn't stand arguments."

"Is that right!"

The doctor wrote something on a piece of paper and stood up to leave.

"You didn't tell me why he had a stroke, doctor."

He handed her the piece of paper, "Here is the death certificate. It doesn't have the proper seal. I'll have to come back with my stamp."

He walked towards the door. Hormat reached into her bag to take out some money. "Doctor, how much do I owe you?"

"Nothing."

"Why doctor?"

"It's just not necessary. I'll go get the stamp. They won't accept it without the seal."

And he walked out the door.

Hormat went to the closet to pick out a black dress. The black and violet silk dress looked better on her than her other dresses did. But no. She put it back and decided to wear a more simple black dress. The sound of the doorbell startled her. She thought, *that's probably Adam's mother, Laiya.*

On her way to the door, the lump in her throat was beginning to well up. As soon as she opened the door and saw Laiya standing there, she burst into tears as she threw herself into Laiya's arms. "See what he finally did to himself? I kept telling him not to smoke so much! I kept telling him he would have a stroke finally. He never listened."

With dry eyes and even drier mouth, Laiya stared at her. She was dazed. Hormat was afraid the poor woman was about to have a heart attack.

"Try to calm yourself, mother! Just let yourself cry, like me."

"Where is he?" Laiya asked.

Hormat pointed towards the room upstairs. "In his room."

And she carried on crying, "How he loved his room! He never left his room at night."

Leila moved towards the upstairs room while Hormat went back to her closet to remove her colorful clothing and dress in black.

The doorbell rang again. "It's probably Nazafarin." Hormat had called her right when it happened. "Why are you here so late?

Friends should be right by your side in times of need."

She was crying. She was wearing a black dress, and had on a black chiffon chador. "Why so late? Because I was dyeing my hair." And she pushed back her scarf, "This color looks better with black."

"I wish I had also...nevermind. Come in. Why are you standing there in the doorway? Adam's mother is upstairs. She just arrived."

"Where is Roya?"

"I sent her to school. I thought her seeing all the crying and grief wouldn't be good for her. I didn't let her think he was dead."

"Well what will you do eventually? She will have to know sooner or later."

"We'll deal with that later... now you go upstairs. Did you call everybody?"

"I called whatever numbers I had. Well, I didn't actually call. I gave the numbers to Parviz and he called everybody. I was too distressed. Besides, my hands were stained with haircolor. Everybody will be here soon."

She had to finish getting ready before everyone arrived, and she had not yet eaten breakfast. She also had to light the samovar for tea. "The guests will perhaps want tea or coffee."

She turned up the fire under the samovar and went back to the door to welcome the other guests. "Let's keep the door open."

"Oh, Aunt Baunee! My child's father is gone! The light of my home is…" and she burst into tears.

Standing in the doorway, Batool began talking, "I say it's the evil eye my dear! I have always said so. It's only been ten years since you married a handsome husband who was genteel and sophisticated. Don't think I'm biased because he's my nephew. It is a fact everybody knows. It was clearer than day that sooner or later he would be jinxed and fall to death. How I urged you to get him an amulet!"

She wanted to say, *I got him one* … But she stopped herself and said: "Come in, please."

༄༅

The fortuneteller had said: "Your husband is young, handsome and full of vigor."

Hormat said, "I know."

"But you are cold."

"I know that too."

The fortune teller warned, "He may leave you for the first person who shows him affection."

"I see."

"Don't you want to show him love?"

"I don't know how to," replied Hormat.

"Then others may ..."

"That's why I'm here."

"To cast a..? On you? Or on him?"

"On him!"

"Should I block him?" asked the fortune teller.

"Yes, block others from him, and block him from others."

The fortuneteller stared at the floor.

"If you change your heart, it would be better than ruining others."

"I can't. I've been trying for a year."

"He is a good man. I don't want to ..."

"I'll pay whatever the cost."

"I don't want his money."

"I have no choice. If you do a permanent job, I will come every month and make payments to you."

"This thread has 86400 knots. Sew one knot to the inside of his pocket every second for a whole day and night so it will not show."

❧❦

"Why don't you come in?"

"I feel so terrible for you. You're in shock my dear aunt. Try to let your feelings out; you'll feel better."

"I do try. Go ahead upstairs. Adam's mother is there with Nazafarin, my friend."

As soon as her aunt climbed the stairs, she darted back into her bedroom to get at least her black scarf from her closet and cover her head. She stood in front of the mirror. She felt that her black scarf did not look right with her yellow and orange shirt. She saw Nazafarin standing behind her in the mirror. She turned around; her eyes were red and puffy.

"What are you doing, Hormat? At least come upstairs for a little while. They are killing themselves with grief. Bring them some tea or at least something to drink."

"The doorbell is ringing."

"Oh, I forgot to leave the door open! Nazy dear, by the time you make the tea, I'll be there."

"But I ... I think you should come."

"Attend to the guests, Nazy dear! I'm not myself."

She ran to answer the door. When she opened it, she froze in her place. It was the fortuneteller, standing there all disheveled and agitated. Her white hair was sticking out from her scarf, and her eyes were bloodshot from either crying or a lack of sleep. She had always come across so cool and self-confident.

"I can't do it forever, darling. It has to be done every month."

"I will. I'll do whatever you say.

"I'm also giving you a bit of fat from the wolf's muzzle. You should dab it on his clothing - the clothes he wears to go out."

She was frightened, "What will it do?"

"Make his male friends avoid him so he will be exclusively yours."

❦

She preferred not to ask her in while her aunt and Laiya and the others would be there. She spoke to the fortuneteller with desperation in her voice, "Forgive me for being so late this month."

Worry and urgency wavered in the old woman's eyes.

"That's not why I'm here."

"Then why?"

"Where is your husband?"

"Why do you ask? Has anything happened?"

"Last night he came to my dream. He killed me a thousand times and each time brought me back to life."

"How?"

"How? He was a heart. A big heart with eyes, ears, hands and legs."

"No, I mean how did he come to you?"

He asked me, "What have I ever done to you?"

"To me?" I asked him, "Nothing."

"What wrong have I done to anybody?"

"Nothing."

"Why did you do this to me?" he asked me.

"I am a fortuneteller..."

"Is your job to torture the spirit? All I ever yearned for was to love and be loved. All I ever wanted to do was love others and do good to them. What sin was there in that?"

"Sin?"

"Then, why did you take these from me?"

"Your wife ..."

"She is damned to hell. But why did you let her ruin you as well? Why did you send yourself to hell by your own hands?"

"And he showed me. It was a valley of molten fire. Its fuel was composed of human bodies and stones that burned. They were all there; all the people for whom I had done sorcery. You also were there. Fire blazed from all parts of your body."

She felt like fire was flaring from all the organs in her body. Her legs felt weak. She leaned back against a column to keep from falling. She was completely at a loss for words.

"Now ...?"

"Now I want to get that damn amulet back from you."

Hormat thought she should say something.

"How much do you believe in dreams? They say a woman's dream is always inverted and opposite."

The old woman became even more agitated, "Let me come in!"

She pushed Hormat out of the way, closed the door behind her, and put her basket down, pulled open her headscarf and revealed her neck to Hormat, "See! This is no longer just a dream. I was hung up in that hell from a molten ring; the ring of damnation."

Around her neck was a blistered, bruised, infected red mark.

Hormat felt dizzy as the room began to spin. She let out a blood curdling scream as her knees folded and she fell to the floor.

The doctor looked up at Laiya, Aunt and Nazafarin, "I've never seen anything like this before. She is showing no signs of life, yet her body is as hot as an oven."

The Wedding Shower

A letter from Cyrus

My dear friend,

I hope you won't be too surprised by my writing to you after so many long years. During this time I have not been disconnected from you, as I have been following you through your books and writings. What motivated me to copy your address off the back of one of your books and write to you, is an unfortunate event that has recently changed my life. I thought that if you could write this story with your skillful hand, many people could benefit from the useful lessons in it. And some others would be put in their places.

I have written the original story in my own words and enclosed it in this envelope for you to read. I hope that you will agree to polish the story and heighten the impact of the message it carries.

Before I forget, I should tell you that I have always looked with contempt upon the couplet by Hafez that reads, "It was best to leave all – and hold to the tresses of the beloved" thinking that if a drawing were to depict this couplet, it would definitely show a bunch of slackers each grabbing and pulling on the hair of their mistress!

But now that God is putting me to the test, I understand what Hafez means - that people should be content with one wife and refrain from pursuing others. I see firsthand how the events of everyday life push mankind towards spiritual wisdom.

Anyhow, please read the notes and if you have any questions or problems, please write to me at my office address.

By the way, you can contact me at this telephone number Saturdays, Mondays and Wednesdays from 4-6; this is when my wife is at the fitness club. Please do not call other than at these times.

Explanatory note:

My friendship with Cyrus dates back to 15 or 20 years ago; that is, we were friends all throughout high school. We both were in the same class and sat at the same table. Although our major of study was mathematics, we were both interested in literature. Our literature class was very special for us even though he occasionally would get on our lovely teacher's nerves with his heavy and ridiculous comments and views.

I saw this interpretation of the Hafez couplet in his notebook. It reminded me one of his literature classes.

The teacher was explaining a Saadi poem of rhymed couplets - two-line stanzas; the main theme was fervent love, both between human beings and between human beings and God.

"What shall I scatter at your feet for you to love? One cannot speak of head and heart what value they have!" She explained in her interpretation of the poem that the poet considers even the offering of his life for the beloved as merely a pittance.

Cyrus stood up, asked permission and spoke (he always expressed his views firmly and in a self-righteous manner), "I think the meaning of the poem is that the poet is telling the beloved *not* to speak of head and heart because they are off limits in their amount of worth. He is asking what he can offer his beloved *beyond* these! That's why the statement should be followed by a comma after *one cannot speak of head and heart*."

His tone had gone from confident and self-righteous to pompous when the teacher finally yelled, "Sit down! Who do you think you are giving the lecture here? No, just get up -

get up and get out! And don't come to class tomorrow either. *Just get out ..."*

I was to a great extent reserved and introverted while he was a cheeky extrovert. We were such opposites that everybody was amazed at how we turned out to be such close friends. He was known for playing practical jokes on people so well that they wouldn't even know they were the brunt of the joke until much later on.

Of course, I was always watching out not to be a victim of one of his own jokes. I knew that it didn't matter to him; he would play them on friends as well as enemies.

After we got our diplomas, I went into literature and he went into accounting. I had pretty much lost all touch with him until this recent note.

When I read the note, I remembered his personality and all the stories from back then and wouldn't put it past him to play a trick on me after all these years. But when I read his writings saw the energy and life in them, I felt I wanted to get to know him again. When I looked into the events of his life more deeply and found out how the years had gone by for him, I felt truly sorry.

In his note he had added that there was a cassette recording of the incident and that if I wanted, he would send it to me. For the story to be entirely documentary I decided not to establish telephone contact with him and instead wrote a letter to him as follows.

My Note to Cyrus

Greetings to my dear old friend,

Receiving a letter from you after years of being out of touch was surprising and wonderful, and at the same time disappointing and sad in that I was sorry to hear about your unfortunate story. But it is something that has happened, the past is past and life goes on. I will do my best to write your story so that others can benefit from its message. I would like to receive the cassette that you mentioned. The more information you provide me, the better you will help me document your story. If you think of anything else I should know about, please write to me. I look forward to seeing you again soon.

Cyrus's letter:

I have enclosed the cassette with this letter. Although I have the original in my possession, please try to keep your copy safe because no matter what, it is a private, family affair and God forbid it fall into anyone's hands. The reason that such a recording exists in the first place is because of the mischief and betrayal done to me by my wife, Manijeh. She made the recording to document my pleas. When she left the house, she forgot to turn it off. If any questions arise or you find any ambiguities in the cassette or in my writings, please write to me for enlightenment. (Although I am myself burning out like a candle and am making my last sputters). God bless you.

My Explanatory Note

When I listened to the cassette in full, I arrived at the conclusion that most of the other notes were unnecessary and redundant and it would be more expedient if the cassette were simply transcribed and put at the disposal of the reader. I decided to extract any necessary information from Cyrus's notes and insert them where necessary in the transcript. Meanwhile, after listening to the cassettes one or two letters were exchanged between Cyrus and me as you will see. As the recording was recorded from outside the bathroom door, the audio is naturally inaudible in some parts where I have marked with successive periods.

My last point: my intervention is to the extent that I have rendered the broken and colloquial conversations into written form. That is all.

Transcribed Cassette

	Sound of tap water.
	Sound of a key turning in the lock.
Cyrus:	The door is open Manijeh, but don't bother; I have already scrubbed my back.
Manijeh:	Just wait and see how I tan your hide.
Cyrus:	What kind of talk is that, Darling?
Manijeh:	Whose wedding did you say you were invited to today?
Cyrus:	I said (in relaxed tone) it's that friend of mine who is a writer.
Manijeh:	Don't you think they might have mistakenly written your name as bridegroom on the card?
Cyrus:	(the sound of the water stops) What card? Who gave you permission to search my pocket? (the sound of rushing to the bathroom door and repeated twists of the doorknob) Why have you locked the door? Open it! I told you to open the door! (possibly the sound of soapsuds hitting the walls and the door)
Manijeh:	What kind of idiot do you take me for? Just you wait! I'll make you pay for this.
Cyrus:	(with a tone showing a blend of anger and hatred coupled with affection) Open the door my dear Manijeh. Open so I can explain. It's

	a simple mistake!
Manijeh:	(angry) Go and explain it to your aunt, you scoundrel! I'll show you what a mistake you've made!
Cyrus:	(with the previous tone, a little tenser but with an air of begging) Please Manijeh! You know I'd die for you! Open the door. It's not what you think!
Manijeh:	How naïve I was when I asked where you were going and you said, "I'm going to my friend's wedding." "Where are you going now?" "I'm going to get the invitations printed for my friend's wedding" or "To place an order for my friend's wedding cake" or "To find a venue." Now perhaps you want to take on the role of bridegroom for your "friend's wedding!" Over my dead body! You'll stay right there until I get back. I will disgrace you in front of everyone!
Cyrus:	(with pleading) Where are you going, dear Manijeh. Wait ... I ... I can't explain while I'm standing here naked like this ... Please let me talk to you ... Open the door dear Manijeh ... I can explain everything, but not if you don't open the door!

Manijeh: (from far away) I *will* open it! When I come back, I *will* open it!

Cyrus: Where are you going dear Manijeh? Please don't do anything rash! (Shouting) Manijeh! Open ... the door (sound of the apartment door slamming)

If only this damned bathroom had a window! (possibly the sound of a head butting against the bathroom wall) There was no one to tell me – you idiot! What are you taking a shower for - exactly two hours before the ceremony! There were so many places you could have taken a shower! Anywhere but here! Why did you have to go and take a shower at home? What a stupid move! Would the world have come to an end without a shower today? (a repetitious sound of pumice stone hitting the head) Let all the pumice stones of the world shower on your head for ruining six months of effort by one small mistake. To hell with the six months of effort! You spoilt a life time of your credibility! Oh my eyes are burning! I've got to rinse my head. Look at your face in the mirror; all foamy and white like a 70 year old man with the tears trickling down your face! If they didn't know better, people would think you're weeping! (Sound of showerhead)

Damn it! If this card hadn't fallen into Manijeh's hands, everything would have been perfect and you'd be blow drying your hair like a brand new groom rather than sitting in this dank prison wondering what to do, hiding your tears under a shower of water! You would have been pinning the boutonniere on your suit right now!

Oh, cruel world! Oh, damn fate! Oh, destiny! Why have you all suddenly decided to conspire against me and wreck my reputation? You were all working *with* me. You all were doing just what I wanted. Why are you all suddenly my enemies? Why did you all save the other side of that coin for tonight - on our wedding night that is waiting for me, a night that is nothing less than a kingly night? (Sound of water stops)

Why didn't you expose me earlier on? Were you choked and unable to speak when I was proposing to her? Why didn't you say something before I threw away all my money? Why didn't you trash my life while I was buying the fruit and wedding pastries? Why didn't you show yourself when I was hiring the bride's hairdresser? Why didn't you motivate my wife to steal the card from my pocket when I was doing everything in the name of my writer friend? Why did you leave everything to be destroyed at the last minute when I was just a few steps away from the altar? Why didn't you send her to search my pocket when the bill from the jewelry store was in it?

Oh, it's getting so cold. Could that coward have switched off the heater before leaving? (Sound of shower) Where has she gone now? Who will she be coming back with? I'm sure, she has gone to bring her father and mother and brawny brothers. To hell with them! I'll show them! I haven't committed murder. I haven't broken into anyone's house. I was just getting married. I have a wife, yes – so be it! Those who have a one-story house build another story on top of that! There's nothing wrong with it! The foundation should be solid, which it is! Nowadays, so many people are even building houses with *several rooms* all on the first floor! Nobody objects to them! But now that it's my turn, the world has come to an end?! The difference between me and others is that the rest of the world acts in secret and sneaks around about it, but I build my house right out in the open. Why don't they just fine me? Why destroy the house? Idiots!

I've got so much money invested in this plan. Just today look how much I spent on the construction permit, the siding, paint, painting and decorating; and how much money I spent on her hairdresser, the marriage license, and her dowry? Nobody thinks of all these! (Sound of water being turned off and teeth chattering). Why did this damned water get so cold? (Sound of the front gate opening)

They're here. I hope it's her relatives. If it's my father and mother I won't know what to say to them. (a thunderous sound of the

front gate slamming closed) Too bad I'm nude when I ought to have a shield, a coat of armor, and a helmet - otherwise... (Sound of key being turned in the lock, the door opening, and a high, feminine screech-like chorus) Damnation!
(My explanation: It is clear from Cyrus's other notes that the aforementioned band consisted of the bride, the mother of bride and the bride's aunt)
Oww!! (the sound of high-heeled shoes hitting against the wall of bathroom, storm, thunder, a bulky body falling on the ground)

End of cassette

Letter from Cyrus (Supplementary)

You may not believe if I tell you how that the innocent-looking Manijeh did a 180 degree turn around and set the whole world ablaze with her fury. In a flash she had grabbed the car keys out of my pocket, went to the reception hall that was written on the wedding invitation and asked them which beauty parlor the bride was using that day. (As is custom, the groom picks up the bride from the beauty parlor and takes her to the reception hall.) And here I was locked in the bathroom - wretched and broken! And Manijeh drove the car decked with flowers to the beauty parlor. She told the bride that she was my distant relative and had come on my behalf to transport the bride. I found out this story later. She picked up the bride, as well as her mother and aunt from the beauty parlor and started driving towards our house. On the way, she told the bride calmly that the groom was still in the shower; she said they would pick up the groom together before going to the ceremony.

To avoid bothering you with all the gory details, the whole time the bride didn't know that Manijeh was my wife. Manijeh played it cool and did not insult her or use bad language against her. She told her it wasn't her fault. She said that both of them were being cheated on. She explained that we had been married for ten years that we had gotten married here in our house. Manijeh announced, "Your Mr. Groom is a second-hand groom - and a refurbished one at best!"

As a rule, they should have gotten out of the car right then, but they didn't believe her. They insisted that they wanted to see the groom who was locked in the bathroom; and of course this was what my wife wanted as well.

Exactly at the same moment I was cursing myself, heaven and earth, I heard the sound of footsteps approaching. Imagine, standing stark-naked in the bathroom and suddenly the door opens and you see your wife, your bride-to-be in her wedding dress, your mother-in-law wearing heavy make-up and a strange woman, eyes popping out of her head, all lined up in front of you. What would you do if you were me?

The best thing to do in a situation like that would be to pass out. And that's precisely what I did. Right when I saw a white, high-heeled shoe coming at me, I placed my hand over my heart and fell on the ground and fainted - or at least *feigned* unconsciousness. When the bride saw that I was knocked out of the ring, she directed her figurative punches at Manijeh and yelled, "You clueless bimbo! Why don't you control your husband?"

And in that artificial coma I was in, I could hear Manijeh not retreating, "How the hell would I know that he has descended upon you? Unless you wanted someone else's man, shouldn't you have done some investigating to see whether he has a family or not when you were asking about his background?"

Sobbing, the bride asked, "Weren't his father and mother and family killed in an earthquake?"

And Manijeh turned to me, the unconscious, and said, "You bastard! In their sight, you have killed all your relatives!"

And still sniffling, the bride said in my defense, "Now what are you abusing this poor unconscious man for?"

And with that, to say Manijeh "lost it" would be an understatement.

"There you go, that's right, pushy broad! No need to play innocent. Only God can protect us from you! Laying claim to my life even before you step your dirty foot through my door! If I hadn't interrupted your plans, you would definitely have been riding me like a mule by now. Hurry up! Get out! Out! Out! The show is over!"

Although I turned my unconscious body towards the door in order to eavesdrop on their conversations, I still could not get much. Apparently, my mother-in-law had fainted near the door and Manijeh helped them out the front door to avoid having to answer for a dead body on her hands.

(End of Cyrus' note)

My Letter to Cyrus

I listened to the cassette and read the notes. I'd really like to know how you are doing now. And what Manijeh did to you after that event? I'm imagining that her next step would have been to file for divorce and by now you'd have gone your separate ways. Anyhow, I am eager to know the rest of the story, not for me but as a lesson to serve the readers.

In the meantime, I hope that I'm not that writer friend whose fiancé you wanted to marry. Do give explanation in this regard.

Letter from Cyrus

Unfortunately, I must admit that I have had no other writer friend except for you. You will definitely be upset knowing that have burgled your name, but I hope that I can make up for this. And now about my current situation, about which you had asked.

After that heart-rending event, Manijeh did not only *not* separate from me, but surprisingly continued living with me wholeheartedly. As a consequent, she starting controlling me so that no one else could ever tear us apart - I mean me, and our life, from her hands.

The story hasn't been all that sad up to this point, but what is excruciating and sorrowful is that at present, I have been turned a little lamb (my explanation: in editing, I should have used the term "sheep" rather than the childish term "little lamb" but since sheep does not convey the intention of the protagonist of the story, and in order to show the depth of the disaster, I will keep the term "little lamb"). It is an understatement to say that I was a little lamb.

After that incident, Manijeh bought a time clock to record my departure and arrival from work by punching in and out – like the kind installed in offices. It is good to know that it was paid for with the money I had saved for my honeymoon with the bride-to-never-be. Now I register my exit from the office at 2:30 and my entry at home at 3:00 p.m. The extent I fear the machine at home I do not fear that of the office. The main cause of my fear is that Manijeh has not so far disclosed our story to anyone; she has in lieu of that, kept the wedding card like the sword of Damocles.

When I rarely forget to punch in and out or something is wrong with the machine, she reminds me of the card in a consistent tone. The association of this card with the wedding card subdues me and strips me - and all of the organs of my body - of any unauthorized movement.

At present, I turn over to her at the beginning of each month all of my pay along with a copy of my paystub and she in turn hands me a fixed allowance to cover my taxi fare to and from work. The reason she requires me to give her a photocopy of my paystub is to ensure that she won't be uninformed in case I get a pay raise, depriving me of any possibility to save the difference for future wedding ceremonies. But in all fairness, she is not too hard on me and isn't stingy when it comes to household expenses. A few days ago when I had felt like having roasted rice and almonds, she bought it and brought it home for me the same day, and let me eat as much as I wanted.

I now understand that if she put her foot down about my eating too many dried, sour cherries, it was for my own good so that I wouldn't get a belly ache. When she occasionally deems it advisable, we even take a trip, and I can enjoy being away from the city and breathe the fresh air and even buy a souvenir.

By the way, I was about to forget to mention at after that event she had a baby to make me more committed to our marriage. In other words, I mean we had a child together. Now, a large amount of my time is spent attending to the affairs of the baby. Things are good. Fatherhood is not bad. He is a good child. I was up all night washing ... (note: this part is omitted for preserve the pleasantness of the story.)

At present, although I have completely forgotten how to drive, have regained my health because of walking, as she is the only one who can use the car. Of course, if I want to go to the doctor or take the baby to the clinic, she will drive me. She believes that I don't need a car and that having one might lead me off the straight and narrow path. She thinks I might give a lady a ride somewhere just to be nice, and that might lead to other things.

Anyhow, I am now fully satisfied with my wife and am enjoying the joys of family and hearth.

My letter to Cyrus

Salutations,

Last night when I was reviewing the notes for the umpteenth time, I noticed that the story lacks a main element essential to a story and that is what your incentive was for marrying another wife. It is not necessary for me to explain to you that in a story, if the incentive of the protagonist for taking a certain action is not clear, the structure will be weak and the events befalling the protagonist will seem unreal and not believable. I look forward to receiving your prompt reply.

Letter from Cyrus

I'm not sure what you mean by protagonist or weak structure and other such terms, but in one word I can say the reason was *idiocy*. That is all.

My Letter to Cyrus

Dear friend,
     Please give me a more in-depth answer. It won't cost you anything! In fact, I already guessed that idiocy was behind it but I was hoping for a more detailed and precise explanation of your motivations. Idiocy is a general concept, but there are elements and reasons for it. As long as these are not clear, the reader won't be able to come to believe your actions. Anyhow, the creation of a good story hinges upon the clarification of your incentives. Good day!

A Letter from Cyrus

     Apparently you are more impertinent than I am! Now, if I said something out of formality or self-deprecation, does that entitle you to take advantage of it and seek the details? If that is the case, I warn you and your *curious* readers ... (note: I have used the term *curious* in place of the disrespectful term "nosy" in the original) that whether you and your readers believe it or not, it has no impact on the story and makes no difference to me either. It is an event that happened in broad daylight and brought about dire consequences. So what's the use of knowing the incentives?

Basically, if you really want the final word on this, there was no idiocy about it at all; it was a shrewdness and astuteness in the full sense of the word; only a small mistake in computation spoiled it. Imagine! If that historic and at the same time careless mistake - that is, taking an untimely bath - had not been made and my plan had been carried out in full, wouldn't you and your readers have said *bravo* to me? You would have! Definitely, you would have, particularly if you knew that prior to the event, Mrs. Manijeh had full confidence in her cleverness and precise control over her husband and bragged about it everywhere with friends and relatives. She had sworn that no movement of her husband was hidden from her eyes and that her husband was like wax in her hand.

Therefore, to enlighten you, let me explain that my move was not at all inspired by an incentive to marry a second time. If such was the case, I would have swum underwater like many others do without creating as much as a ripple in the water! So if I pursued my plans to hold the ceremony out in the open, it was because I wanted to send a message to my wife and all the other women in the world that controlling another person is no way to have a relationship. (Note: this sentence is cliché and worthy of removal)

    I planned to drive the bride through the streets in a car decorated with flowers, along with family and friends honking horns; a ridiculous thing that I did not accept to do in my first marriage. Then I wanted to stop by my house in the bridal car, and run upstairs to check in and come right back out. All for the purpose of demonstrating that obligation in a marriage should be emotional and voluntary, not physical or mandatory - as in hiring detectives or using a computer! (Note: readers can take this sentence as the moral of the story because there will be no other moral to the end).

    Now go and sit and write. I think that with so many incentives even four stories can be written! I wish you success.

Cyrus' note: (on the back of the paper, small and illegible)

    I write these few lines furtively for you because I feel you are very simple. The story is not as intense and severe as I have written in these notes. I added fuel to the fire to teach your readers a lesson. I'm not on the right track as much as perhaps you and Manijeh thought. It is for some time that I have become acquainted with a girl at the bus stop. We sit and talk on the bus going to and from the office. In the meantime, since the telephone at home is blocked, she calls me on Saturdays, Mondays or Wednesdays between 4 to 6 p.m. when Manijeh is not at home, and we talk over different issues. Of course, on one or two occasions Manijeh called home from the club and demanded to know why the phone was busy. I told her that the receiver was accidentally off the hook, whereas I had done it on purpose. See what I'm talking about? Now you go looking for incentives! Here they are.

My Final Note to Cyrus

As you may know, stories are the essence of man's existence; they are a limpid and transparent reflection of reality and any artificial touch will only serve to reduce their value and wonder. Accordingly, I preferred to transfer your painful, inspiring and instructive narrative exactly as is to the readers only changing the names; and only in critical cases have I added explanations. I have co-mingled the transcription of the cassette which you kindly sent to me into your narrative. At present, I am deciding whether or not to preface the story with this sentence: "Any similarity in this story between Cyrus and Saeed Jabbari is purely coincidental." Of course, it doesn't make much difference. We writers normally insert sentences of this nature at the beginning of our stories and books to relieve the pangs of conscience as well as any possible consequences.

Santa Maria

I was inspired to call her Santa Maria from the first moment I saw her. I don't know why this name suddenly crossed my mind. Some time ago when I had journeyed to the San Marco Church, I heard this name in the Christian prayers; upon hearing this name, all of the purity and pleasantness of the holy Mary instantly settled into my heart.

However, as the years went by this name and memory completely faded from my mind - until she appeared. There was no real connection between her and the holy Saint Mary, the mother of the Prophet of Mercy; yet when I saw her I felt subconsciously that no name could conjure up that purity, congeniality, spirituality and beauty all together and to this extent for me.

I said, "Would you let me call you Santa Maria?"

She smiled. Her hair was smooth, long, and chestnut brown. Her eyes changed colors in the different light; sometimes they were brown, at other times green, and yet other times blue depending on where she looked. She had a small and trim nose on top of her beautiful lips. Reddish-brown eyelashes protected all the beauty of her eyes like an umbrella. When she smiled it seemed like small jasmine buds blossomed. You couldn't take your eyes off of her beautiful pearly teeth.

She wore a long, blue silk dress that spread before her like a cobblestone path.

I thought I had seen her many times before in my mind's valley, but she had never seemed as real, present and lovely as in this meeting. She would appear, move my heart and then leave. She would never stay long enough for me to have a chance to tell her how desperately I had been seeking her.

She now asked, "Now why Santa Maria of all names?"

I replied, "I don't know."

And after a brief pause, I gazed into her eyes and continued, "But if a mirror were to be placed in front of that heavenly Mary on the earth, wouldn't you undoubtedly be the clear image in that mirror?"

She said: "I pray your horizons will always remain heavenly. Will they?" She didn't wait for an answer, but started walking on the sand. Perhaps she wanted me to see the wind blowing in her hair. Each step she took would leave behind freshly sprouted grass in her footprints, and white blossoms would instantly bloom.

I said: "I've grown so tired of the deception and manipulation. I have always searched for someone who wasn't so earthly."

I saw her silhouette as she sat down on a tree stump. She looked at me askance, "How heavenly are you yourself? How heavenly is your heart?"

What could I have said? I said, "To the extent that while I breathe upon this earth, this earth is too small for my heart."

I wanted to ask her, "What about you? Where are you from? Where have you come from?"

From where I was sitting, the ocean was spread out before me and the woods at my back. I thought she might have come from where the woods meet the sea, or from the mountain tops or from in-between the interlaced trees, where women from Galesh suddenly come into sight from in-between the raspberry bushes with purses hanging from two sides and occasionally children tied on their backs ... but ... she did not bear the slightest resemblance to the Galesh women.

Her figure was graceful and lithe, her skin as clear as a lily and her hands as delicate as wings. She could not have come from the sea. No mermaid would ever favor human beings like this. But, no human being could ever resemble a mermaid this much, either.

I said, "This crystal isn't from around here."

She smiled.

I said, "Nor this pearl."

She said, "What an expert you are on the region's goods! A businessman, are you not?"

I said, "People wouldn't buy my goods if I gave them away!"

She said, "No one wants a heart. Don't sell it."

I said, "I won't."

She said, "Don't even put it up for sale. Breakable goods are safer in the warehouse."

I said, "Even if it withers in there?"

She said, "It won't, for crystal doesn't wither."

I said, "You are more of an expert on goods than I am!"

She laughed.

And a sweet scent like acacia wafted through the air.

I said, "What would it be like if you were always with me - smiling? I imagine the earth and sky would be filled with the fragrance of acacia!"

She said: Enjoy the moment - which is fleeting like the clouds."

And she looked at the sky where a white cloud moved across the sky above our heads. Now I could see the entire grace and virtue of the sky in her blue eyes.

I said, "How can beauty and chastity be reconciled?"

She said, "These two have always been together since the beginning, but in order to rule over them, some people created disharmony between them."

I asked: "To rule over…?"

She replied, "Both beauty and virtue."

I said, "Then you're from the very early days because you command both features."

Perhaps to be nice, she said, "You want to see me this way."

I said, "No, my eyes see what they see, and are only interpreting you."

She said, "If you imagine a treasure in your mind, you will eventually lose the treasure because it is a figment of your imagination."

I said, "…"

Before I could say anything, she rose, I presumed to leave and my heart collapsed. I took a chance and said,

"Would you let me love you?"

She smiled, stood with her back to me, and gazing at the horizon, said, "How wisely you step out in search of love?!"

I said, "..."

Before I could say a word, she went on to say, "You don't want me for me, you are merely seeking the fulfillment of your needs in me, your ideal desires, your unattainable desires. You came to me once before in the story of Mahjabin."

I thought for a moment I was about to faint, but instead fell to my knees on the soft dunes of the sand. She did the same and we were knee to knee and breath to breath.

I said, "But Mahjabin was real."

She said, "Am I not?"

I said, "Then you were also Mahjabin?"

She said, "Yes! And Shakiba too."

I said, "Why then did you leave me?"

She said, "Why should I have stayed with the superficial descriptions you made of me in your stories? They were merely material aspects, lines and moles, eyes and brows – of which plenty can be found in the streets and alleys!"

Unwittingly, I said, "People see only the outer form. You are beautiful both form and depth of meaning."

An ambiguous sorrow played in her eyes like a thick fog covering the woods. And she said, "So where is that depth of meaning in your writings?"

I gasped. I seemed to be speaking from the bottom of a well. I could hardly hear my own voice. "You know better than anyone that I am not preoccupied with the outer form; but I have not found any words to express the inner soul."

With a firmness that seemed impossible from such grace, she said, "Well, don't come to me again until you have found expression for the inner meaning of a woman. Otherwise, you will beat me down with your material expressions and earthly explanations, and your writings will squander me."

She stood up, shook the grains of sand from long gown in the air. As she shook her long, blue gown, a storm raged and the sands flew; the sands rose from the ground and blew into my eyes, and I could no longer see her.

The Last Defense

The judge is settling into his soft, swivel chair. He takes a deep breath and says, "The charges state that the defendant, Basem Rahmati - son of Hasan, without premeditation or motive, thrust a kitchen knife into the abdomen of his wife, Manijeh Sabeti. If the defendant or his lawyer has any objection, they may offer it in their closing argument."

One member of the court audience shouts, "What defense?! A murder so transparent stands in no need of defense!"

Sitting behind this person is the deceased's uncle. He shouts, "Where in the world is a murderer and criminal protected so much?" so indignantly and violently that the defendant, meaning Basem Rahmati - son of

Hasan, turns around and says to him coldly, "Please shut up."

In order to prevent continued discussion and debate, the judge raises his hand with composure, and gaveled three times firmly on the bench.

The defense attorney gets up to stand at the podium, however, the defendant, Basem Rahmati - son of Hasan, takes his hand and pulls him into the chair, and instead, he himself rises confidently to the podium. He has a tall, slender body, disheveled hair turning gray on both sides of his forehead, with a soft, sparse beard which needs to be trimmed.

It is obvious he is trying to look calm, but the sorrow which is evident in his eyes betrays him. To make sure that his voice will be heard, he blows a few times into the loudspeaker and then begins.

"I am on death row and I accept this fate, but I have a few important things to say based on reason and logic and I won't let you execute me until I have my say."

The uncle of the murder victim shouts: "You and reason?! If you ..."

The judge strikes the gavel on the bench and the defendant, Basem Rahmati - son of Hasan, answers the man coldly, "You were supposed to be silent; what happened then?"

The uncle of the murder victim turns livid and stands up shaking his finger. Before he has the chance to utter, "your forefathers ..." the judge strikes the gavel on the bench and shouts "Silent!"

And the defendant, meaning Basem Rahmati - son of Hasan- carries on, "You're making a big deal over nothing. After I'm gone you'll have plenty of time to argue. It is me who needs to have my say as soon as possible and then be delivered to the gallows. After I'm gone, you can set up courts and give as many speeches as you want, and I'll have no objection! Of course, rules dictate that I remain seated and allow the respected attorney a chance to speak. Obviously, he is more articulate than I am and makes better arguments ..."

A self-satisfied smile appears on the defense attorney's lips as he stands up, nods his head in appreciation and sits back in his chair.

The defendant, Basem Rahmati - son of Hasan, goes on to say, "But the reason I did not let him speak this time was that he does not convey *my* intent. Your honor and the audience both know better than I that lawyers often get paid to create confusion between right and wrong."

The defense attorney blazing at the insult, stands up and shouts, "Judge, sir, I have stated before that the defendant is crazy."

The judge gives no answer. The defendant, Basem Rahmati - son of Hasan, goes on to say, "Attorney, sir, don't cause yourself stress for no reason. You'll get paid whether I am convicted or acquitted. Therefore, let me speak my peace. Regarding lawyers, let me add this point that the job they do is truly difficult. Having perfect command of the nuances of laws and the ability to bend the rigid articles and amendments in any direction they want and at the drop of a hat - *and* getting completely opposite results from one fixed law on different occasions is not a simple task! But the reason that I did not let my defense attorney speak this last time was that I did not intend to be acquitted. I thought it would be better for the truth to be known than for me to be acquitted. Here you are! A perfect trial slogan: *It is better that the truth be known than for the defendant to be acquitted.*"

The defense attorney and the judge laughed at this comment the most. The convict, Basem Rahmati - son of Hasan, goes on to say, "The thing I would like to scrutinize is the final statement made by the court, *The defendant, Basem Rahmati - son of Hasan, without premeditation or motive, thrust the kitchen knife up to the handle into the stomach of his wife, Manijeh Sabeti.* This confession has been accepted by my defense attorney. However, the favor they did for me was to say that the defendant, that is I, while the crime was being committed, was experiencing a sudden burst of rage. May you be sacrificed for your aunt! Is this logical?! If such were the case, each and every murderer could have been acquitted because of *a sudden burst of rage*!"

The criminal lawyer stands up angrily and yells, "Objection, your honor, sir, how do you permit such a lunatic to waste the court's time like this?"

The judge strikes the gavel on the bench and says calmly, "Overruled. The court must permit the accused to enter his closing argument."

The defense attorney sits back. The convict - Basem Rahmati, son of Hasan - continues with a sneer, "Obviously, the attorney is completely in the right. If I had not admitted to the murder, the attorney could have settled the problem in a different way. He has no other choice than to call me crazy. This is what he told me."

When the defense attorney stands up to protest, the judge gestures him to be silent.

The defendant - Basem Rahmati, son of Hasan- takes out a cigarette from the pocket of his cream and brown checkered uniform, but out of respect for the court places it back into his pocket and continues what he was saying.

"The privilege of this state is that based on the physician's diagnosis of my manic outbursts, I will be admitted to the hospital for a while. When I recover, I will be discharged. That is surely better than execution! But what remains untold in the meantime is my story, and what goes to waste is the truth."

The defendant's father - Hasan- stands up in fury and walks towards the podium and takes the defendant's hand -Basem Rahmati- and while dragging him back to his chair, shouts, "Your honor! These words indicate that this boy is mad. This madness is not only recent; he has been this way since childhood."

The murder victim's uncle protests in a hoarse and broken voice, "Let the defendant have his say; it is his inalienable right. The defendant, Basem Rahmati - son of Hasan, turns to the victim's uncle and says, "I am amazed at how you have not yet shut up; we came to the conclusion a half an hour ago that it would be better if you did so."

Then he lets go of his father's hand, kisses it and says, "As always you only want what is best for me, but let me speak."

He continues, "I said that I have something to say about each word in the charges. If at least one word in that sentence had been correct, a person wouldn't feel so bad. More than all, these two terms without *premeditation* or *motive* burns one's heart. *The defendant - Basem Rahmati, son of Hasan- has without premeditation or motive...*

"Firstly, what I did *was* premeditated. It encompassed a detailed and fundamental premeditation that lasted for three years during my married life with this person, which is no trivial premeditation. If we had not been married, if we had not lived together for three years but instead, for example, I had seen her walking down the street and suddenly did something like that, one would say unpremeditated ... exactly like our marriage! I can accept *that* being unpremeditated, but not *this*. Does the court believe that three years of living together is too little premeditation for such a move?

"Secondly, was I crazy to do such a thing without a motive? When one drinks a glass of water, there is a motive; one drinks to satisfy one's thirst. How is it possible for me to have done something like that without a motive? I will speak more about this premeditation and motive later.

"You have cited *kitchen knife*. If God has not given you intellect, He has at least given you eyes. You might at least have opened them so as to tell the difference between a hunting knife and a kitchen knife. But now that you have not noticed that difference, I will explain it to you. You see, a kitchen knife is a tool with which one cuts meat and chops vegetables, peels eggplant and potatoes, and wedges watermelons and honeydew melons. But a hunting knife is a knife for hunting, beheading and peeling the skin off of animals. The suspicion I encountered regarding the deceased forced me to use a hunting knife. I wasn't peeling a potato! So that is another mistake.

"Now regarding the kitchen knife or any other knife you have cited: *Up to the knife handle into his wife's stomach* ...It is good to at least be fair. Let us suppose you do not differentiate between the function of the stomach and the heart. For instance, your heart functions as your stomach or vice versa, but you at least cannot deny the spatial distance between the two. The heart lies at least 20 to 30 centimeters above the stomach. The location of the injury is in the heart of the victim. The knife was removed from her heart, yet you cited the stomach in the case file!

"Above all, the phrase *up to the knife handle* is disingenuous. Whoever has seen this knife knows that it has a blade 30 centimeters in length of which only seven or eight centimeters were blood-stained. Is it possible for a 30 centimeter knife to be thrust *all the way* into the chest or stomach of a person but only seven or eight centimeters of the knife to be stained with blood? Does this conform to logic?

"But one can spare all these arguments. That which cannot be ignored is that the murder has been pinned on me. Although it is true that I am an agent in the murder, the actual killer is the deceased herself. In other words, the deceased has committed suicide."

This argument causes uproar in the court and the judge pounds the gavel on the bench and shouts. "Silence! Silence in the court!"

Then he turns to the defendant and says, "Can you prove that claim?" Someone in the audience cries out, "Sir, he is denying everything!"

The defense attorney turns to the audience and says, "Let the defendant have his say!"

The defendant, Basem Rahmati - son of Hasan, tells the lawyer with a smile, "It appears that the argument is new to you. Is it not?" Then he continues, "My main and crucial point here is what I said before: *the deceased has killed herself*, but of course, through me. If this question is explained to you, all other issues including the premeditation and motive of this murder will be clarified.

"My wife, Mrs. Manijeh Sabeti, was 28 years old. She was a French language teacher. She was an accomplished seamstress. She was an excellent chef. She was a good housekeeper. You know about all these. But there was one talent that she did not have, and that one thing, was something you know nothing about; namely, the capacity for love and affection.

"Our life in these three years was like two strangers living in a hotel. Our relationship was like the relationship of two roommates with each other; two roommates who have implied mutual obligations. One is bound by this unspoken contract to pay the rent, buy the groceries, and pay the water and electricity bills and the other to teach at school from morning to evening and in the evening do the housework and leave the remaining chores for the other to do, exactly like the distant, formal dynamic that roommates have with each other.

"Of course, when I say *we* were like this, even that is wrong, because *I* was not like that and I could not never be like that. When I came home from the office at night, I saw that the table was set, the tea was ready, the fruit was placed on the table, the ash tray was clean, but the lady of the house was asleep, because she had been at school all day and naturally couldn't be expected to fritter away her time at that time of night, 8:30, for me. Therefore, she had eaten her dinner and gone to bed. The only time when she didn't eat and go to bed early was when she had papers to grade. But in her attitude toward me, it really made no difference.

"This was what our nights were like. In the mornings, she would wake up, have her breakfast and leave before I woke up, because if she didn't leave the house by 6 a.m. then she would not get to school, which was clear across town, by 7:30 a.m. So she couldn't help that.

"I thought I might be the cause of the problem for coming home so late. So for some time, I stopped accepting overtime work and got home by three o'clock but not only in this span of time did no miracle take place, but in fact the difference in earnings and spending actually triggered new problems.

"I told you these things so that you would be able to visualize the situation, because the problem was not about eating or sleeping sooner or later. The problem was her attitude towards our life together.

"She was a person who attended to her appearance and dress outside of the home, hobnobbed with people and children, but was indifferent to me like a stone, and showed no warmth or kindness at home. I tried everything I thought would motivate a woman's affections, actions that would have tamed a wild animal (that's why I thought that a hunting knife was more suitable for her), but if you imagine that she displayed one iota of reaction to all this love and emotion, she did not.

"If you think that during the entire three years we were married I heard a single affectionate word out of her mouth, you would be wrong. Any words spoken in our house were either about everyday life or her lessons, classes and school. It seemed like from the beginning of our life together, she didn't realize how her actions grated away at my heart and soul. And similarly, I don't believe myself at fault for thrusting the hunting knife into her heart. It was she who from the day we were married, pushed the knife into her own chest with each act of her indifference; with each time she ignored me, with each time she didn't respond to my affections, the knife went a little further in until that night when the knife touched her heart and she died.

"Shortly after we were married, I thought perhaps she did not like being married to me. I raised this issue with her and told her I could not go on living this way. I reminded her that the purpose of married life was to foster people reaching peace and completion, and should be a response to their emotional needs. I told her that our married life was failing to fulfill such needs; in fact, it was having the opposite effect. I told her that if she didn't like living with me, we could separate and each find someone more suitable; thanks to her teaching career, we had never had a child.

"She got angry and started accusing me of wanting to marry someone else. She couldn't believe I had such expectations out of life. For her, feeling love and affection was weird. She believed that there was nothing wrong with her. I had the right to think that in her chest there was no heart.

"Or perhaps instead of doubting about whether there was a heart inside her chest, I could have at least been curious and opened it up with a knife or something to see a whether stone or potato or a beet had been mistakenly planted in there. I did not, God forbid, want to kill her or thrust the knife into her chest out of revenge or hate.

"Now it is upon the court to decide. Despite all these words, I accept the punishment of execution set forth for me. I said these things so that others might take care of their married life; secondly to understand that the court's final charge is erroneous from top to bottom. The murder was not without premeditation or motive; it was not done with a kitchen knife; it was not thrust all the way into her chest to the handle of the knife; it was not thrust into her stomach and killer was not me. The killer was herself. That is all!"

The atmosphere in the courtroom is unsettled. The judge orders silence in the courtroom and then turns to the defense attorney and says: You are right, sir! The defendant is out of his senses … "

This Human Being...

    He showed up one morning and abruptly said, "This human being is exhausted today!"
    I replied, "Is that right? What's the matter?"
    He said, "To tell you the truth, I didn't sleep last night."
    I said, "Well, this poor human being can have a lie-down from now until midnight and get some rest."
    Stretching, he said with a yawn, "That's the whole point. I can't. If I could, I would."
    At first I thought he might be trying to pull a fast one on me again, but then I felt he was holding back something serious and was just looking for an excuse to say it.

I busied myself turning the pages in my text book and asked, "Why can't you sleep? It's not as if you're under a lot of stress from work."

He took a key out of his pocket and twisted it around in his right ear, cleaned the earwax off and said, "Not from work. To tell you the truth, last night my wife died. I wasn't able to sleep because I was busy making preparations for the funeral ceremony until morning, so I couldn't sleep."

I said, "Farid! Don't say things like that! It's not even good to joke about things like that!"

He said, "And it is even worse when they are true; it's so sad. She was a good wife. Last night I was on the verge of tears a couple of times."

I said, "You mean you *didn't* cry?"

He said, "I controlled myself."

I said, "Now I'm sure you're just messing with me. But God forbid, and may I be damned if she does die, wouldn't you cry?"

He smiled sarcastically and said, "What a jerk you are! God has *not* forbidden and my wife *has* died; she died last night, I'm telling you!"

Then he reached into his pocket and took out a piece of paper and showed it to me, "Here is the death certificate!"

It reminded me of Mrs. Manijeh, the crazy, old woman in our neighborhood. Around two and a half a years ago she waylaid me one morning and said, "My husband died!" And she let out a sidesplitting laughter. But Farid had not gone mad.

I said, "Farid! For God's sake tell me you're not serious!"

He scratched his bulging stomach and said, "I'm dead serious. Unfortunately, it's true. You don't joke with people over other people's lives."

I said, "So what are you doing here now?"

He said, "I've been busy. I woke up before sunrise and took care of everything."

I said, "So why are you acting so normal? You're acting so cool!"

He said, "I can't kill myself over this! But I'm as sad as can be. I really couldn't eat breakfast this morning. I mean there was just no time. Now if you have anything, I would love a bite to eat."

I remember when his father died; we all naturally rushed to his house to express our condolences and sympathize and our express our sorrow. He was sitting in a special place reserved for prominent people, and nodding acknowledgment to friends coming and going. As dictated by duty, we attended to the guests all morning. But he didn't budge an inch from his spot and then voraciously ate two plates of food at lunchtime. To all the people looking at him in amazement he said, "Stress gives a person a big appetite!"

I said, "Why then do grieving people grow thinner with each passing day?"

He said, "Because the nutrients aren't being absorbed in the body. The stress doesn't let it happen."

I said, "I'll make something for you then." Then I remembered, "By the way, what about your wife's relatives? Have you informed them?"

He said, "She didn't have much family; she only has an elderly aunt in Shiraz. I wonder if she is even still alive."

I said, "Death is really a simple thing, isn't it?"

He said, "Yes, as long as it concerns others. But for the one who dies it is not. Then death is a difficult thing."

I said, "Well, what happened that your wife suddenly ... suffered this state?"

He said, "She died giving birth last night; rather than giving birth, she died."

I said, "What about the child?"

He said, "He died as well. The poor child! I was devastated. What about you?"

I said, "Sad? I still don't even believe it."

He said, "What kind of man are you? How come you don't believe such simple words?"

And then he took off his socks, lay down on the sofa and said, "What was I thinking when I chose you to go to for comfort? I thought a friend who was single would understand me better. Such problems are not very easy for married friends to digest. Not all are as patient and forbearing as I am. Obviously, by a fluke, my wife died on a night when you would be home the next day."

I said, "Well, what do you want to do now?

He said, "If it's okay with you, I'll make myself something to eat."

Then he got up to go into the kitchen. I stood up and made him sit down, saying, "No, it is not good for you to work in your state. Sit here! I will make you something myself."

And he happily reclined close to the telephone and said, "Okay. Then I'll make some phone calls."

I had not yet completely chopped the tomatoes for the omelet by the time he had already submitted the full obituary to the newspaper.

I heard his voice from the kitchen. With messy hands I came out of the kitchen and asked, "So you set the funeral ceremony for Thursday?"

He stopped dialing the number to answer my question, "Yes, I am off on Thursday so I can be there. I think that day will be good for others too. When the obituary is published in the newspaper tomorrow morning, which is Wednesday, anyone who wants to can read it and attend on Thursday."

I said, "Many people may not read the newspaper. How are you going to inform your close friends?"

Again he took the receiver and while dialing said, "I'll call a few of them, and I'll have you call a few others, and you tell them in turn to inform still others."

I said, "What about the seventh day ceremony after her death?"

He said, "We won't hold the seventh day ceremony. In three or four days, I will submit a notice to the newspaper announcing that the expenses for that ceremony will be donated to charity. The maximum amount will be five hundred tomans."

I said, "The cost of the ceremony is only five hundred tomans?"

He said, "No man, the charge of the newspaper announcement. It doesn't oblige anybody."

I returned to the kitchen to finish making the omelet. He first called Mahmoud's office. Before the other side picked up, he yelled, "Are making the omelet?"

I said, "Yes. Don't you want me to?"

He came up to the kitchen door, "Yes, I do. I wanted to say not to forget the onions. Make it with onions."

I said, "Oh my poor grieving friend!"

Feeling a little sheepish, he replied, "Onion has nothing to do with a funeral or a marriage ceremony. My breath won't smell bad. By the way, there is plenty of time till Thursday."

I went back and got busy chopping the onions. Ms. Manijeh, the neighbor, was also busy cooking, and she called out from her kitchen window in that girlish voice of hers – that you wouldn't believe was coming from a woman of her age – "Mr. Javad! Do you have any onions?"

I said, "Yes, sure."

And I tossed two onions over to her, both of which she caught in mid-air. Their kitchen was two meters away from ours. She always left the window open and threw her food scraps out into the backyard of the story below. In response to the protest of others, particularly those on the first floor, she would say, "Whoops! The maid is to blame. I'll fire her soon and hire an obedient maid."

Again, Farid called out, "Javad! This Mahmood does not believe me. You come and tell him."

Mahmood had a right not to believe him; even more than the current coolness Farid was displaying, his bad record incriminated him. Once he had invited many of us with our wives and children for lunch. When we reached his house, we were met by a closed door with a note on it that read, "Due to my relocation from here, there is no one at home. Please do not knock on the door."

And we were all embarrassed and ashamed in front of our wives and children, and went home disappointed. And when the guys protested later he said, "Forgive me! It was too bad that happened, but during that two or three day period, I had found a cheaper apartment and moved there quickly. There was no opportunity to call you. The next time something like that happens, I'll definitely ..."

And I had replied, "I'll be damned if I trust you a second time!"

I wasn't sure whether this was another one of his tricks or if he was serious. However, evidence indicated that the problem was serious. I took the receiver and told Mahmood, "The issue seems to be serious. I also looked at the death certificate and overheard his phone calls about the obituary. Now if you don't believe him then wait until tomorrow. If the obituary is published in the newspaper, then do come; otherwise, forget it."

Mahmood insisted, "If you help me rest assured, I will come."

I said, "Assurance? I cannot rest assured even after the funeral ceremony as to whether Farid has something up his sleeve or not."

And then I felt the sting of Farid's slap on the back of my neck. He took the receiver from my hand, glared at me and told Mahmood, "How come nobody believes me?" And I didn't hear what Mahmood told him that made Farid grit his teeth and reply, "Okay, wait till *your* wife dies. Watch and see if I come to the funeral ceremony. I won't even say a prayer for you!" and he hung up the receiver and told me, "What a trap I'm in! Does a person have to be given assurance by force to come to a funeral ceremony?"

He then asked for the telephone numbers for Masoud, Bahram and Ramin and I gave them to him and went back to the kitchen. I couldn't hear their conversations over the sound of the frying onions but when I was finished making the omelet and placed it in front of him he said, "I did it! In addition to the three, I also called Cyrus. Masoud was not available. When I told his wife, you should have heard how she wept. People are real actors! *My* wife has died, and someone else's wife overflows with tears!"

After wolfing down a few bites of the food, he said, "I've got to do something about this; I'm all alone."

Despite the fact that it had not even been one hour, I was fooled by him again. I was thinking that perhaps he had something important to say. I asked with curiosity and concern, "What do you mean?"

As he stuffed in a bite of food too large for his mouth, he said with difficulty, "There is no *'what do you mean'* about it! I have been alone, living without a wife since last night!"

He emphasized "since last night" in a way that you'd think he meant that ten years had gone by. And he carried on saying, "One cannot live without a wife. Now, if you are a bit geeky and waste your time on studying and college, it can be overlooked, but when I think about who will be there as of tonight to make my food, wash my clothes, clean my house and many other things ... I see that one truly cannot live without a wife. I am sure that if you didn't live near your parents and you could afford it, you'd have married a dozen times by now."

He sopped up the oil on the plate with his bread and put the last bite in his mouth, wiped around his lips with his finger, licked his finger and said, "If it was possible to find a good wife in one or two days ..."

Disgusted, I interrupted him, "Wait at least until your first wife's burial shroud is dry."

He calmly looked at his watch and said, "It is close to 11 a.m. It will be dry by now, especially under the sweltering sun in the cemetery."

While picking his teeth with a toothpick he found on the carpet, he said, "You probably have tea in the house, am I right?"

I said, "Yes."

And I went towards the kitchen. Despite the fact that he knew I could hear his voice, he almost yelled, "By the time you come back with the tea, think of who might be a good marriage prospect for me."

And after a brief pause, he went on to say in a louder voice, "Thursday there is a ceremony to mourn the deceased. Nothing can be done about it. If possible, it wouldn't be a bad idea for us hold a brief marriage ceremony and get it over with."

While the kettle was heating up, my eyes fell on Ms. Manijeh who as usual was standing in front of the broken mirror in her kitchen troweling on make-up. She was in her 50's or 60's, slender, and frail with one foot in the grave. She had inherited the house from her husband and her children had deserted her because of her dementia. Only occasionally did they pay her a visit or bring something to her. She was squandering her late husband's meager pension buying make-up and cigarettes and she was often at a loss on how to provide for her meals. She would put on weird clothes, change her hair color every day, smoke foreign cigarettes, put on heavy make-up, and answer people's questioning looks by saying, "Today or tomorrow a suitor is going to come for me and take me away with him."

When she saw me in the kitchen, she came to the window holding a bottle of foundation in her hand and asked, "Do you have any cigarettes? The maid has gone to buy some but hasn't come back yet."

I said, "Sure, just a minute."

And I got two cigarettes from Farid and threw them into her kitchen window. She cast a look at the cigarettes and said, "In return I'll give you some name brand, foreign cigarettes this afternoon."

I said, "That won't be necessary."

When I brought in the tea, Farid was standing in front of the mirror combing his curly hair. He also combed his moustache, sat down and said, "Well, did you think of a good match for me to marry?"

I said, "I did, but marriage is not something that can be done at no expense, especially with the costly dowries –"he interrupted me and said, "Don't worry at all.

To be honest, I've got a new job and I can afford a million high dowries with ease, but more about that later. You'll see when it all happens."

Such remarks made by him were believable; despite the fact that he had never held down a steady job, his income was double all of ours.

Just two years ago I saw him enter into rental agreements with five separate people over his rental property. He collected a deposit of a hundred thousand from each of them, promising to give possession of his property in three months.

He invested the five hundred thousand and in three months earned more than one hundred thousand on top of his original investment capital. He then returned the money to the five would-be renters and backed out of each deal using a loophole in the contract.

The reason he did this was not at all based on need; as he put it, "I only wanted to put them in their places."

One time we were sitting around and I heard him say he could easily earn forty thousand per month, but didn't have the patience to do it. And when the guys messed around with him, he said, "I will show you that I can in exactly three months to this day."

I now replied, "If you are prepared mentally and have no problem financially, well …"

He said, "So, you've got one up your sleeve?"

I said, "There is this lady in our neighborhood …"

He couldn't stand it and interrupted me again, "Well, well? What's she like?"

I said, "Of course, she's not a virgin – she's been married once, but she's vivacious. I've never seen her without make-up. Meantime, she owns a house; she will rescue you from tenancy."

Full of excitement, he said, "So, why are you still sitting here?"

I said coolly, "I've already spoken with her. I did it right when you asked me to think of someone."

He said, "So, I guessed right. I was about to doubt my own ears. When you were in the kitchen I heard you talking about courtship, etc. So, you have mentioned it? Okay? Okay? When are we supposed to go talk to her?"

I said, "Right now."

Pleasantly surprised, he said, "So, you finally agree that once you make up your mind to do something, you shouldn't pussyfoot around about it."

I said, "Anyone who associates with you would come to this conclusion."

His laughter filled the air as he said, "I never thought anyone could be as clever as I am!"

I said, "It happens but rarely."

He said, "You should come with me to meet her."

I said, "I'll come just to introduce you two to each other. The rest is up to you. I am neither a reverent, white-bearded figure nor do I have the slightest experience in these things. Anyway, I'm expecting a phone call, that's why I can't stay there long."

"Okay!" he said, "I'll take however much of your time you can give me."

And we left. He was going over his reception plans on the way, "Friday is good, from six to eight…no…then it will fall into the dinner hour. It would be better to have it from five to seven, at the girl's house."

I said, "What if you don't like her?"

He said, "What kind of talk is that? A morsel you find for me?"

I rang the doorbell and after a few minutes the door opened and the first thing that caught our attention was Ms. Manijeh's strong red lipstick and golden thinning hair decorated with two red combs, a long red skirt and white pearl slippers. She smiled with her whole face and body and gave signals by winking. Both of us were open-mouthed. Farid's amazement was at her appearance and my astonishment was how she could have made herself ready in such a short time.

We said only, "Hello!"

And Mrs. Manijeh said, "Hello! Please come in. I'm so honored. Thank you for coming. How are you? Please come in!"

We went inside and I saw the bewilderment and confusion in Farid's face gradually fading to contentment and satisfaction just as he openly tried not to lag behind Ms. Manijeh in the verbal small talk in the time it took us to reach the living room.

"Thank you. How are you? I beg your pardon if we've come at a bad time." At the threshold of the room he whispered into my ear, "What a kind and cheerful mother she has!"

I said, "You ain't seen nothin yet!"

His satisfied smile broadened his moustache as he said, "Is that right?"

I said, "Of course! Believe me."

When we sat down, I opened up with, "The integrity of human beings these days has become so flimsy."

Ms. Manijeh nodded and Farid did too, although he wasn't really listening. He said, "Yes, that's true."

And I continued, "There are people who still haven't buried their…"

Farid squeezed my hand and grit his teeth, meaning for me to keep silent.

So I kept silent. Farid made small talk about the weather until Ms. Manijeh made a cordial apology and left the room to bring tea.

Farid gave me a nudge and said, "What a scumbag you are!"

I said, "Sorry! I didn't mean any harm."

And then he calmly whispered in my ear, "We have nothing to talk about with her mother; why doesn't the girl bring out the tea instead?"

I said, "I told you she was not virgin."

I said, "What do you think so far?"

He said, "Excellent! To tell you the truth, I always wanted to marry into a classy, high caliber family. With a mother so kind, courteous and high class at her age, the girl is definitely worth considering!"

I said, "That's right. Really!"

He said, "Now, do you think her mother will want to live with us?"

I said, "Ask these questions yourself. I have to go."

When Mrs. Manijeh entered, I stood up to leave, but before saying good-bye I told Farid in a loud enough voice for Ms. Manijeh to hear, "If you want, you can arrange for the wedding ceremony on Friday."

And Farid said happily, "Certainly! Certainly!"

And I apologized, excused myself and left the house but I did not go home. Visualizing Farid's furious face after a few minutes caused me to stay away from the vicinity of the house and not return until evening.

In the evening when I got home, one of the neighbors who was also a student at my school, saw me before I opened the front door and said, "Excuse me, right before noon a man came looking for you. He was very angry. His forehead was bleeding and the back of his skirt was torn. He was knocking frantically at your door but you weren't home. He knocked harder. I told him that if you were asleep you would have woken up by now. I told him you were definitely not at home. Then I went to bring him some tissue to wipe the blood on his forehead. He asked for safety pin and I gave him one. He also took out a piece of paper from his pocket, wrote a note on it and slipped it under your door.

I said, "Did he ask you to tell me anything?"

He said, "No. He didn't even say thank you."

I thanked the boy and apologized and then went inside. The note was right beside the door. He had written with a bold, angry, shaky hand: *You have no feelings! You don't even have a heart! You bastard! You good for nothing! You play with people's feelings and affection. From now on we are finished. Signed, Farid.*

And then slightly below that in smaller handwriting he wrote: *This human being got his payback today.*

Dead in the Water

If you don't rush me, if you don't interrupt me, if you don't divert my attention, I will tell you all the details of the story myself from the very beginning to the very end. I've heard what she has to say before. Don't believe her! If you wring out her argument like a rag, not a drop of reason will trickle out. You all heard how she spent an hour concocting so many cockamamie stories! How many of them actually had any substance? That's why I remained silent. I let her present her ideas in full, so that nothing would be left unsaid. Therefore it is only fair for her to keep quiet now and let me make my case. Once I've had my chance to speak, there will be no need to give me the third degree. You can read between the lines. In the meantime, if you think any part of my speech irrelevant, don't interrupt me. I will get to the point in good time. In return for your consideration, I will do my best not to take even half the time it took for the opposing party to make her case.

Anyhow, the story that brought us to this juicy end, began with a simple wink. I was standing in for my father at his shop. I was just busy selling goods like a gentleman without thinking about anything mischievous. My father had gone out to buy wholesale merchandise for the shop. On these occasions when he would go to market each week, he would always send somebody to his shop to keep the doors open so the customers wouldn't go elsewhere.

That day it was my bad luck to be standing in for him. This lady came in to buy buttons. I thought we didn't have the right buttons that would match her dress, but what could I do? I couldn't lose customers. She was carrying a red sweater in her hands. She placed it on the counter and with a fabulous wink, she said, "I would like some buttons."

However hard I strained to figure out the connection between the buttons and her eye movement, I was at a loss as to why a person who wanted to buy buttons would do this with her eyes. I pointed at the boxes of buttons on which samples of each button had been attached. I said, "These are our buttons; which ones would you like to look at?"

She did that with her eye again and said, "I can't do it this way. I need to see up close." When she said this, I became certain that her eyes had a problem. Her eyes did this strange thing when she spoke, and she also wasn't able to see a button well even at such a close distance. Otherwise, seeing a button wouldn't require a person to move up so close. Besides, the boxes of buttons had been placed where the customers could easily see them and select from them.

To make a long story short, the issue of the buttons gradually turned into my standing in for father at his shop the next week as well in order to prevent the loss of customers. The situation carried on for several consecutive weeks until I don't know what the neighbors told father, but he took me aside one day and said, "Now that you have been so good to me, you could help me even better by going to the market once a week and letting me take care of the shop instead." No matter how much I insisted I could run the shop more efficiently, he refused and withdrew me from this good job.

My future appointments with this lady for transactions of the heart were outsourced from the shop to the parks, cinemas and the streets.

(If you are getting tired, be patient; I will try to summarize the rest.)

What was so strange to me from the very first day was the sudden passionate love and extraordinary interest she had in me. Her admiration for me tempted me to erroneously assume her opinion to be right about what she said about me. But when I was alone, the thought would occur to me that if I am really so good, extraordinary, excellent, handsome, kind and what not, then why don't others notice this too and treat me in a way deserving of such majesty? Well, it was natural for me to think that the only one who appreciated me with all these extraordinary features was her ladyship, while the rest were senseless and dim and neither had the capacity to understand what love, feeling and emotions were, nor could comprehend the dimensions of character of such an extraordinary man like me. This is why I became gradually, or rather swiftly, taken by her and turned away from all others.

And I, in order not to leave her affections unanswered, I added something to them as interest and returned these affections to her. Let me say outright, I admired her beauty, elegance and kindness no less than she admired me. The reason for so doing was my own naïveté. I did not actually want to tell a lie. I thought I was more or less right in my admiration for her. In retrospect, it was like someone had drawn a curtain over her evil deeds and dressed up her good deeds which were either nonexistent or very few in number. I was so happy I couldn't be bound by earth and time. I was deeply in love with her.

One day after preparations that are requisite to such talks, she said, "Can you imagine what a wonderful feeling it is for a woman to be waiting at home for or her husband at night and for a man to know a woman is waiting for him too?"

I, the senseless, only said, "I have never had that experience, so I wouldn't know" but I neglected to ask how *she* knew that this feeling was pleasant. The problem is that she did not make this remark only once; she repeated it so many times that it aroused my curiosity to perceive such a feeling. On the one hand, with the preparations that I previously mentioned, my assumption was that if there was one person in the entire world who could understand me and was qualified to be my wife, it was undoubtedly her ladyship.

For this reason, I ran the risk of talking to my father about her. I asked him to come immediately and write up the contract for this lovely merchandise. My father, who was an experienced businessman and knowledgeable in life and society, naturally could not accept her so simply, and he raised issues using logic that refuted a thousand arguments given by inexperienced youth like me.

He believed that anything called love at my age was meaningless. He believed that at my age, a person would even fall in love with a wall if it leaned toward the person; even if the leaning of the wall was due to an earthquake. He said that if I waited a few years I would laugh when looking back on these days. He said I would come to realize that these years marked the outburst of phony and wishy-washy loves. However, I was determined to prove my love to her, what I now realize was a very baseless and wishy-washy love that was blinding me.

As such, I saw no choice but to enter the arena through the window of sentiments and so I did. I assigned my mother and sister and others the task of arranging for the wedding. I set about convincing my father by pretending that my very existence depended on a string that tied me to this lady and if this string were cut, my life would be over. Let me emphasize that father and others were all rational and reasonable and I was a numbskull who refused to listen to anybody. Despite his discontent and all the trouble, father acquiesced. The wedding ceremony finally took place and all the papers were signed.

Now from here on is where the story gets interesting. What I have told you thus far was just to set the stage so you would understand the story in context. And will the court please tell this lady not to kick her foot against the table like that – she is racking my nerves.

By the way, I forgot to say that before we signed the marriage certificate, my father and mother explained the groom's situation in detail to the bride's father and mother. For example, they made sure they understood that the groom did not yet have a good job, had not completed his military service, and did not own a house, among other things that I don't remember now. But I remember that my parents told her parents that the only things that made the groom earn a high school diploma in the first place were the beatings and lashings he received from his father, and that God only knows where he got so much talent in the affairs of love! The bride's mother assured them saying, "We do not want the groom for his money, position or education. For us the important things are his humanity, his personality and his good qualities that we see in your son."

May I bury this mother and daughter with my own hands if I tell a lie! They said these things and addressed me with such affectionate terms that I felt like my own perfection was overflowing and leaking out from me!

In a nutshell, after the ceremony was over and the dust was settled; I mean the day after the marriage certificate with her ladyship was signed, she said abruptly, "You see, all this talk about love, affection and so on was right for when we were courting. But the realities of life are something else. Once married life has begun, these words should be put away and buried, so that people can survive in life."

"His complaint is baseless, your honor!"

This was the gist of the remark. Now, I may have transposed the expression a bit when relating it. I wanted to say to her, *What? You married me by means of these words. If anyone is supposed to be buried, it is you who should be buried for teaching me these words. What did poor, pitiful I know about love anyway?* But I didn't say this. I thought I had better wait and see how the situation would unfold.

The next day or the day after, I don't remember precisely, her mother turned around and told me, (I mean perhaps she didn't literally turn around), but I remember she told me, "Life has its basic requirements. Man cannot live on love alone. If you know of a good, lucrative job, then go to it. If not, then Sima's father's office can give you so much work that you will be able to earn your livelihood through it. But a person must have a strategy in life. You can't just go along like before. This young, new bride who is training to get her driver's license will soon require a car. It is not the duty of the bride's father to buy her the car; you are the one who must provide it. How will you do that? Nobody knows. Let us suppose that your father buys her the car, but even so, life is not just this one car! Life has thousands of costs and requirements."

I wanted to say, *My grandfather would turn over in his grave if my father ever bought this imposter a car. If he had the money to buy a car, then...*

I thought, *Oh, why are they getting angry over nothing?! I did not say these words!* But I thought I should just grin and bear it and see how things went.

One or two days later I don't know how, but the subject of having and raising children with this lady came up. She put her foot down saying, "Let me tell you right now that I have no interest in raising children! Why do you think there are so many nursery schools around? To raise bottle-fed babies until they reach elementary school age!

I did not let her continue and said, "Well, it's a long way off until the time comes when we have a child." But what burnt my heart the most was the reply she gave, "Well, don't say I didn't tell you beforehand!" Don't laugh if I tell you that she played that same game when it came to housework. "Truly, I am can't stand to do housework! I wasn't made for this kind of work. We should think about hiring a maid around here. People can't live without a maid, can they?" I wanted to say, *You profligate! Did your father or mother have a maid that you expect to have one right from the start?* However, again I said nothing; I told myself to wait to see what happened.

Could someone please tell this lady to sit beside the heater if she feels cold, so that she won't rack my nerves by gritting her teeth so much?

Everything that I have just told you about, took place over a period of time less than one week. One year after the signing of the marriage license, we were to hold the wedding reception before carting the body of the groom off to the new house.

Their clumsiness was in that they did not think to inject their demands of me little by little over the course of one year. That very first week they accelerated so fast that they themselves lost control of the vehicle.

On the eight day, mother and daughter launched the attack together. The mother said, "Have you ever looked at my husband's life?" The daughter said, "Have you noticed what a comfortable life my sister's husband has provided?"

The mother said, "Do you know where the success of my husband lies?" The daughter said, "Do you know to whom my sister's husband is indebted for his peaceful and happy life?"
Both said together, "In one word, obedience - obeying one's wife!"

Believe me, your honor, that if you were in my shoes, you would have lost your patience and smashed up the café of life! Well, I also did the same.

I said, "Pack up your freak show and get lost!"

They were shocked. They were not expecting all my silence to result in this. I furthered their astonishment and said, "If you want a lamb, I am not your man. If you're looking for a mule like my father-in-law or brother-in-law then you've come to the wrong place!"

And they say I insulted them. They mean that one word I said. But in fairness, can that one word be considered an insult? A mule is not really a bad animal; it works hard, carries loads, is absolutely submissive, protests at nothing, and observes nothing. These are not bad qualities. I only said I am not that like that. Then I told this lady, "You buried the foundation of love and affection after we signed the marriage contract, are unable to raise a child and you hate housework. What use are you? You good-for-nothing!"

You tell me if this statement is really insulting. If you can think of any better response than the one I gave, then please let me know.

Tell the mother of this lady not to whisper in her daughter's ear so much and not to teach her so much ill will. Whatever we suffer comes from her mother. Well, what came of all these arguments?

The result was that I left their house on bad terms and said I would never set foot into their house again, so that that my life that was about to be ruined by them would be saved. They couldn't believe it. They thought I would return. They must have thought a woman has the power to seduce man to his own doom, but they learned otherwise. One day, two days, one week, one month, two months, one year passed and they realized things were serious.

That woman, her mother, called me and told me in no uncertain terms, "Go and find a house and then come and take your wife home!"

I said, "What? Didn't we have an arrangement to live in my father's house?"

They said, "No, we've changed our minds."

I said, "No problem. I changed my mind a long time ago about the whole thing."

They did not get it at first, but later I made them realize that their actions and words had had a very negative effect on me and made me adverse to women and married life in general - of course, adverse to her type of women.

Well, our story up to this point is not very unusual. Such things can always take place in anyone's life and result in separation or what not. What is strange and unusual happens from here onward.

Three days after this phone call, around 10 at night, I was sitting at home wrestling with my nerves when I suddenly heard the doorbell ring. By the time I got up to answer the door, I heard another sound. It was the shouting and crying of a man and a woman from whose quarrel these words could be discerned, "Oh, people! This young man is a fraudster! He has ruined our daughter's life! He has brought dishonor upon our family! If he did not want a wife, why did he propose! Oh, God! What disaster was this to befall us! Oh God, why did You get us entangled with this charlatan? These people are not entitled to be treated well. You do a good deed and give your daughter like a bouquet of flowers, to someone who turns out to be a shirtless nobody who torments you! Oh, you good-for-nothing nobody! You aren't worthy of marrying into a prestigious family - why did you not sew your coat according to the amount of your cloth? Let all the people in this neighborhood know what sort of charlatans they are living amongst!" and many other words which I don't remember now.

When I opened the door I saw two officers standing at the door and the bride, her mother, her brother, and her sister's husband were standing in the alley – and each were busy making speeches. The commotion they were making caused the neighbors to come outside, each trying in their own way to silence them.

My mother, sister and father tried to rush out the door but I stopped them and pushed them back into the house and said, "I brought on this hell myself. Let me deal with it!"

I asked the officers, "What's going on?"

They presented me with papers indicating that a complaint had been lodged against me, and told me that I should come with them to the police station.

I said, "What for?"

They said, "It's a civil complaint."

I said, "No crime has been committed?"

They said, "No. You are free to also file a counter-complaint."

Meanwhile, her brother and sister's husband attacked me with the intention to beat me. The officers blocked them and said, "Whatever you want to do, do it at the police station!" But all four of them were still busy abusing me with foul language.

The bride was telling my next door neighbor, "This man was not the type to get married. My father was ready to pay him a salary of ten thousand tomans per month, but he is not yet ready to come and take me!"

Our simple neighbor said, "Perhaps, there is something wrong with you!"

And the bride became even more furious and said, "You are all alike in this neighborhood. You are low lives!"

Our neighbor whispered in her ear, but I could hear her voice. "He has been brought out here for no reason. You would react the same way if you had been insulted like that. That poor fellow is not at fault! He was insulted and he reciprocated with a slap. Leave him alone why don't you? Basically, the whole neighborhood knows you came here to sully his reputation."

I told the officers that I would only accompany them down to the station if they gathered this army in front of my house so as not to create even more of a scene, and silence them until I could go and get dressed and come along to the station with them. When the officers were assured that our house didn't have any back doors, they accepted my terms. I told them I did not intend to escape, that the bride's family had done their job and that now it was my turn. If our house had eight doors, I would not have gone anywhere until I settled my account with that woman and her family.

The officers gathered everyone outside our courtyard wall in front of the house to wait for me while I went inside to get dressed and come back out.

Of course, before I came to the door I did something else – a little trick. I connected the nozzle of the hose to the tap, placed the ladder against the wall, turned the water all the way up and drew the nozzle of the hose up to the top of the ladder which I had leaned against the inside of the alley wall. Then I aimed the water with force at these underhanded frauds who had come to dishonor me.

Of course, the neighbors laughed heartily; even the officers also laughed. But I really did not have any particular intention. I wanted to rinse them and wash them from my life. When you asked me what kind of mess I made, I really don't call this making a mess! If I had actually made a mess, they never would have treated me this way. So what I did had a symbolic aspect. Washing them with water was the polite way of doing what I should have done with them but did not. To be fair, the bad language they used against me was not something that could be washed with water alone! But I saw all of them burning up in anger so I decided to pour some cold water on them to cool them down a little. "Throwing cold water on them" was the term used by the officers. I did not say it. If you ask me, I say they were actually in already in hot water! This small amount of water didn't make any difference; I was simply giving them exactly what they deserved after all the verbal abuse they had showered on me. I did it because I felt that my words weren't holding any water with them.

With the innocence they saw in me they thought they would suffer no consequences if they attacked me with abusive language. Actually, I never thought myself capable of doing such a thing either. Now that it's all water under the bridge, I feel ashamed of myself for throwing the baby out with the bath water and indulging in that behavior.

If in the streets people laughed at them, it is not my fault. If you saw them like that, you would have burst into laughter too. I wish you had seen it. Blush, lipstick, filler, foundation, eye shadow and the like was smeared and running all over their faces and making them look like clowns. If I were in their place, I would have melted into the earth from the shame and humiliation. It was a pity. Before coming here to see you, of course they went to the restroom and cleaned off their make-up.

Now I don't want to stand here in front of you with a sanctimonious air like they did; I only want to warn you not to be duped by their crocodile tears. They take thousands of people like you and me down to the spring for a drink of water and send them home thirsty. You are seeing them now that they're in deep water, but I knew this marriage could not hold water from the very first time I heard their demands. Don't waste your time preaching to them or advising them. You can lead a horse to water but you can't make it drink. Send our case to the justice department and the court to make its decision. Let them go their way and we'll go ours.

Somebody Notice Me!

It's all over. This rope will put an end to all the neglect, ingratitude and thanklessness of all you people. With this red ribbon tied onto it, this rope will admonish you, wake you up and show you what you did to me. You will never understand art – not now or in seventy years! You have no taste or feeling. You will never develop a sense for even the basics of love and poetry. What more could I have done to show it to you?

I toiled night and day, travailed and disbursed my talent and flair just like a prophet on a mission of propagation - of himself, of course. But what came of it? Who among you realized with what a unique gem you are living? Which one of you comprehended what an unrivalled gold mine you have beside you?

I was like a valuable parcel - and I still am - mailed to this world with no recipient's name or address written on the package, which implies that any person could take delivery of me. But which of you treated this valuable parcel the way it deserved to be treated? How much did I urge you to appreciate my value? How many ways and languages did I put to use to get you to notice me? But did you listen? You did not! Now taste the pangs of my absence and suffer the pain of my parting. (What an eloquent verse! If only I had used it somewhere before now.)

Take my father who always regarded free trade far superior to free verse...or my wife who preferred bread to sweet-sounding, succulent verse. Yesterday when I told her I had come up with a new verse she replied, "If you can come up with fresh meat it would be much better!"

It is true that no person can take a mother's place. As long as she lived, I never felt such intense loneliness and solitude as I do now. Although she could not read and write, she appreciated me for my poetry. Never did I recite a verse for her when she did not admire my maternally inherited flair, talent and gift. What would happen if you people had one thousandth of my mother's understanding and feelings?

I won't forgive you. I won't overlook this. You were the ones who said, "Your mother likes your poetry because she is illiterate and doesn't know any better!"

I am therefore taking this historical measure to punish a people who could not understand and appreciate an artistic talent, who was a brilliant figure of the world of culture and literature.

I wanted to state these words as my last will and testament - to be regarded as the last written testimony of this poet - but I will record these words on tape so that they will not suffer the fate of other my other writings - which were snubbed.

O, people! I did whatever was necessary to engage your attention - for you to notice me - but you did not answer my call no matter what approach I employed.

I wheedled my way into the newspapers and they printed my poems, but not a single one of you said bravo to me! Forget bravo! Not a single one of you came up to me to say, "Hey you so and so! What kind of poem is this for you to have published?!" so that I would at least know that one person in the world has read my work. I would be content for my poems to have simply been read, but no one did. No one rang my doorbell, no one stopped me at the corner, no one sat beside me in a taxi or bus to say a word to me about my poems.

It's not easy to get a chance at the podium on poetry night. I had to be persistent and convincing to get the organizers to devote a few minutes to my poem. I was given an opportunity to read one couplet, but I risked the angry stare of the organizers and recited five more poems consecutively - but no sound came from the audience to say bravo or even a dry and deflated whoopee. After the program was over, I walked for one full hour around the exhibition hall but not a single person came up to me to admire my flair and talent or at least shower me with a handful of juicy swearwords.

And that is my case. My neck is in the noose now and I'm one step away from death. When I shove the stool out from under me, it will all be over.

I'm telling you - you people will get nowhere with this attitude of yours! A nation not appreciating its assets and failing to receive its artists ought to be thrown into the trash bin of history. I do not cry; but conscience, equity, mercy and compassion dictated that you should have honored me. As far as I am concerned I was not negligent. It is you who are responsible for whatever failure has occurred.

I even entered politics to engage your attention. I grew a goatee beard and wore glasses but you still didn't notice me. I was pestered by you people who do not know art and do not have the heart to understand!

Residents in the area ought to remember that I walked in the neighborhood streets every day for three full months with a branch of pink flowers in my hand, staring at the sunset, enjoying the beautiful landscape as deeply as possible. I took the hands of two blind people and three old ladies and crossed them to the other side of the street. But no one admired the tenderness of my feelings. No one told me bravo for so much emotion.

I even appeared on television, but the quality of people's greetings in the neighborhood still did not change. Children didn't gather around me and did not ask me any questions or ask me for my autograph. As far as the corner grocer's treatment of me regarding the price of his goods is concerned, still nothing has changed. What else could I have done to get you to notice me?

I composed contemporary verse but noticed that some of you liked ancient poetry better. So I put myself to the task and composed ancient verse as well. But still no miracle took place. I was even forced to inject narcotics in order to inject greater imagination into my verse. I had a pleasant experience but observed no conspicuous difference in your treatment of me. I therefore blame my addiction on you because if you had noticed me beforehand, I would not have gone down this dangerous road and would not presently going through withdrawal symptoms. Everything in this society has mobilized step by step to bring me to this destruction.

    Yesterday I was confiding in a poet who unlike me, was not affected by the pain of public disregard of him. I was telling him all about the grievance I have with society and my cultural and literary loneliness. I had not yet finished my wretched discourse when he interrupted me and said, "In my opinion, your last poem was your most beautiful one."

    "Which poem?" I asked curiously.

    He replied lightly, "The farewell poem."

    And he smiled.

    And I sobbed until morning from all this neglect, ingratitude and thanklessness. There is not much more for me to say as I come to the end of side one of this cassette. I don't feel like undoing the rope around my neck, to come down off the stool and turn the cassette to the other side. There's really not much more for me to say. My last words are that you people have killed me. I blame my death on you directly whether you accept fault for my murder or not.

    If I kick this stool out from under me, this rope with the artistic ribbon on it will tighten around my neck, my head will hang to one side and my legs will dangle like a pendulum, my face will turn purple and my tongue will stick out of my mouth, and nobody will rejoice at my misfortune except you people! This scenario is obviously frightening. Thinking about it is terrifying and it's making my mouth dry, my legs and hands shake and my heart palpitate fiercely.

Maybe I've decided on suicide too hastily. I should have given you people more of a chance. Yes, I should give you a chance, a three-month chance. I shouldn't do anything so rash without even giving an ultimatum first. Life has its sweet moments as well and one should not overlook that matter. Yes...no. Of course, I have the courage to commit suicide. I just think it's better to give the people time to mend their ways and to cherish my flair, understanding and feelings.

Oh, how my legs are shaking! I should untie the rope from around my neck. If the stool, God forbid... from under my feet! Ah! Stool! ... You also re ... move under ... lying support from under my feet ...

Signature

    If no one else believes me, at least you will. You are my mother and you raised me never to lie. You know I have no need to lie. I mean, is honesty supposedly dead? There is so much truth that still needs to be told, why would I tell a lie? But what's the big deal anyway, whether people believe or not? There's no art in them believing what they can see with their own eyes; what is special is faith in the unseen.
    The only thing that is important to me is that you believe in what I say and about what happened. You have been with me from the start. You were by my side through all my highs and lows. You have always known about all my sad and happy times. And you must know about this as well - and believe it.

When our principal said that our report cards had to be signed by our fathers, I raised my hand and asked, "What should those whose fathers are not available do?" He said, "They should wait until their father returns home. Whatever the case, the father is the one who should sign it."

I asked, "What about the mother? Can't the mother sign?"

He got angry over nothing and yelled at me. He thought I was a dim-wit or an imbecile for not understanding such simple words. He verbalized this thought in front of the kids who all laughed at me - but I explained that I *did* understand his words and that's why I asked the question. I may not be a genius but I'm not stupid! That is because I have lived in this world for thirteen years, and earned a pretty decent grade point average in school for six of those years. A dim-wit imbecile cannot study for six years with a grade point average like that. He got even angrier when I said that and barked; "Stupid animal!" and he threw me out of the classroom like an animal.

Our teacher, our cruel teacher just stood there watching and without even saying a word to intervene on my behalf.

When I got home, if you recall, you asked me why I was upset, but I didn't answer you. I didn't want to upset you and I tried to hide my pain, but my heart was truly broken.

It was so broken that crying couldn't soothe it, although crying was all I could do. What else could I do? I went upstairs to the room where Dad's picture is kept.

I took it off the shelf and sat down with it on the floor. I placed my report card before him and said, "Sign it." I didn't say please. I told him he "must" sign it and look at his child's grades, and see what his child has done in the year since he has been gone. I told him that this "must" wasn't coming from me, but was what the school had ordered. I said the school didn't understand plain speech, and so I wasn't going to behave rationally either. I said he "must" sign it. Isn't it true that they say the martyr lives on? Then show me you're alive! Be a father! I could have revealed right from the very beginning that I didn't have a father at home, that he was martyred, and make it easy on myself and the school. But I didn't do this. If you had simply died, I would have done it. But you were martyred and I didn't want to receive special treatment because of that.

I didn't want to benefit from your blood. I didn't want to use your reputation for self-gain. I wanted to be a credit to your name and that is why I tried not to do anything wrong. I never wanted the school to call you about any bad behavior on my part. Then they would have found out that you were martyred, and they might have been tempted to overlook my trespasses and apologize to me. This would not have been becoming of the child of a martyr.

I can't remember what else I told Dad, but I remember that I was crying. I was crying very hard and asking him to look at my grades and sign my report card.

I don't know whether I fell asleep or not, but I sensed a pleasant fragrance in the air which was getting stronger. I couldn't describe this fragrance, Mom. It was a faint smell of rose. It was a fragrance neither you, nor I, nor any other person has ever sensed before. You know how much I love the smell of roses. But there was no comparison of this fragrance with the smell of roses. I don't know what it feels like to be drunk, but I must have been drunk on this fragrance. It was heady.

Then the door opened and a fog-like whiteness like a cloud covered the door. Without touching the whiteness, you could feel its softness.

I gazed at the whiteness. I saw Dad dressed in white standing tall in the doorway, his face glowing like the moon. I don't remember which glowed more brightly, his raiment or his face. I couldn't tell.

The place on his throat that had been hit by the shrapnel was glowing more intensely, as if that spot was spreading the light to his face and body. You've seen the crescent moon in the sky at nights, and how its light glows and spreads around it – dad's throat was like that. Like a crescent, it shined like a necklace.

His face and skin was perfectly translucent, as if even a kiss might stain it. His lips were smiling, like a blossoming flower. There was so much love and affection in the way he looked at me that it brought me to tears; he caused them to flow.

Dad was moving, but he wasn't walking. His movement was more like a cloud drifting lightly across the sky. He came and sat down next to his picture like soft, falling snow. He didn't look anything like his picture. There was a world of difference between the two.

He picked up my report card from the floor and unfolded it as I scooted a little closer to him. He looked at the grades one by one - I could tell he was looking at them carefully.

Then he reached into his long white robe and brought out the pen that he always used to write with. He signed my report card. Then he put the pen back into his robe.

He turned to me and took my face in his hands. He dried my tears and kissed my forehead. I can still feel his warm lips touching me. I kissed that place on his neck – the same place you wouldn't let me kiss before. He smiled when I did that. I felt joyful and content but I didn't cry.

I threw myself into his arms and allowed myself to have a good cry. His fragrance was affecting me. He stroked my head, kissed my hair and rose to leave.

How could I let him leave so soon? I had so many things to tell him about, and I hadn't yet said a word. I grasped his white robe that was softer than chiffon and said, "Don't go, Dad. We need you here."

He took my hand in his hands and said, "You're never alone my dear Maryam. God is always with you. When you're with God you are never alone. I'm not going anywhere. I'm here. I'm always with you. Ask your mother. There's never a night when we aren't together, talking with each other."

I said, "Then please do something about Nahid. She's just a child. She doesn't understand these things. She doesn't even know yet that you have been martyred. She thinks you've gone on a trip. Most of the time, she sits by the front door waiting for you. Every time the doorbell rings, she jumps up and forces us all to come out and open the courtyard door. She is always disappointed because we all don't jump up. She cries and says, "Why are you all still sitting down? My daddy is home! Get up and answer the door!"

Mother gets a lump in her throat as she says, "When Daddy comes home, he has a key. He won't ring the doorbell."

And Nahid stamps her little foot on the floor and says, "His arms might be full and have to ring the doorbell."

When I told Dad these things, tears welled up in his eyes and he simply said, "I know, Maryam dear, I know."

I said, "Dad, when you signed my report card it gave me a sense of peace. I am certain now that you are with us. Please do one more thing for us."

As father looked up in surprise, a tear rolled down his face. He said, "What is that?"

I said, "Sign Nahid's heart so that she can find peace."

Dad laughed in the midst of his tears and said, "God will sign her heart Himself."

And then he left so lightly and peacefully that I missed the moment; the next thing I knew he was gone. I ran to the door and opened it and called out, "Dad, Dad!" The moment he left was when I saw you coming up the stairs.

Now here is the report card, the signature, and Dad's scent. Believe if you will; if not, then don't.

Anahita

The first thing you noticed was her sunglasses and then her plastic grocery bags that she, too tired to carry, had set down on the ground beside her feet.

This left her two hands free to gesture me to stop and give her a ride however far I was willing to take her.

She was standing just past the turn off of the Jahan Kudak Freeway towards Modaress; it was a blind spot for cars coming at high speed, and very dangerous. But I stopped for her anyway. I turned on my blinkers, leaned over the passenger's seat and opened the door for her to put her bags of groceries that she was now picking up from off the ground into the car and then get in herself.

Once in the car, she started warmly chit chatting and complaining about the times we live in and people who won't give a thirty-year-old woman a ride for the sake of decency.

Of course, the part about her age wasn't true. Minus the color and creams she had used on her skin, she would be about forty.

I said, "I can take you to Zafar Street. Then you can easily get a taxi from there."

She said, "Thank you. This is just fine. Especially since it gives us time to get to know each other."

"What?" I said.

She answered, "Yes, sir! My friends ask me why I don't just buy a car since I have the means. I tell them that during the week, the university already provides me with a car and a driver. So why should I give up the one day I have to get out on the excuse of shopping and mingle with people? A person who teaches social studies must get out and be with people, must meet and circulate and live among them.

"Since this opportunity doesn't come about for me very often because of my teaching occupation, why should I deny myself this small amount of socializing? You know? You see, when I leave the house and I'm not carrying anything, I go by bus. On the bus I come up with different social topics to talk about: the elderly, the poor, the disaster-stricken, the handicapped, and the oppressed. I sit by them and start talking to them and when they start opening up their hearts to me, we suddenly realize how far off the topic we've gone. I get energy for a whole week from that one half day."

We were approaching Zafar Street as she kept on talking. I had no choice but to interrupt her and say, "Very well, here we are at Zafar St. I hope you can get a taxi here quickly."

She replied, "I don't mean to be an imposition, but if you could take me a little further to the Sadr Bridge that would be wonderful! If you're not running late already, it would be so nice of you to waste a little of your time for me and take me to that bridge. Then you can take Shariati Street straight back to Zafar."

At my wit's end, I said, "Very well."

She then asked, "Is your office on Zafar?"

I said, "Yes, ma'am."

She said, "Don't forget to give me your address so that I can come over and we can get to know each other in a more casual and relaxed atmosphere. This way is so formal."

I asked, "At which university do you teach?"

She said, "The northwest branch of Azad Islamic University. But which university it is, is not important to me. What is important to me is interaction with the students."

I said,"You must have become a professor at a very early age since you say you're only thirty."

She said, "Yes, I completed most of my education as intensive courses and so I finished it quickly. Then when I earned my Master's degree, I began teaching in that same university."

I pulled over and said, "Ok, we're here. This is Sadr Bridge. Good luck!"

Almost pleading, she said, "Oh, you've been so kind to me. My house is just two streets up. Please do me the honor and take me there so I won't have to hail a taxi for such a short distance?"

I was forced to turn left under the bridge down Shariati Street. She said, "I'll never forget your kindness. I hope I'll be able to repay you soon."

And she continued, "As a matter of fact, there's something I've wanted to tell you since you picked me up but I was afraid. Knowing now what a decent man you are, I know it won't be misinterpreted."

I said, "Thank you. What is it?"

She said, "Today after I did my shopping, I got up to the cash register – please turn right here – and I noticed that I didn't have my wallet. I had a lot of money and checks in the wallet. I had just gotten my paycheck cashed at the bank this morning. I paid the bill at the cash register and came out of the store. Please turn left..."

I said, "I know the rest."

She answered in surprise, "The rest of what? The address?"

I said, "The rest of the address and the rest of the story. You wanted to get a taxi home but you didn't have money or your wallet with you."

I slammed on the brakes and said, "Ok. Your house is right here, is it not?"

She said, "Yes it is." And she opened the car door.

I said, "And you don't have any money in the house? You want *me to loan you* four or five thousand tomans?"

She was silent.

I said, "Excuse me, what is your name?"

She said, "Nooshin."

I said, "Yes, but wasn't it Nahid last time?"

She looked surprised. She said, "Last time?" and she grabbed her bags making ready to get out of the car fast.

I said, "Sit down; I have to talk to you." And I pushed on the gas pedal and made the heavy SUV screech loudly. The half open door was thrown back at her, making her stay in the car for fear her arms and legs would be caught between the car and the car door. She didn't try to open the door again, but she said in a quiet scream, "Stop the car! I want to get out!"

I said, "Wait. You will get out."

She said, "What do you want from me?"

I said, "Just the answers to one or two questions. That's all."

She said, "Then will you let me get out?"

I said, "Why not? What would I keep you for? I have no business with you."

She said, "Then make it quick."

I turned onto the freeway and said, "About a year ago when I picked you up, you were standing there with the usual amount of packages. You hailed me and I pulled over. Of course, I wasn't driving an SUV at the time; it was a sedan. That's probably why you don't recognize me today."

She said, "You're making a mistake. It wasn't me."

I said, "No, you getting rides from people every day might be the one to make a mistake. But I never give rides to anyone so I remember faces well."

She said, "You're insulting me."

I said, "I may do so later, but I haven't yet" and I continued, "You got into my car and told me all these same things with the same exaggeration. On that day, like today, I had just intended on giving you a lift on my way, but like today you begged and pleaded so much that I brought you to this same Anahita alley."

She said, "In this neighborhood, it is possible that..."

I said, "I let you off in front of a house, but after I pulled away, I saw you open the door of a house three doors down."

She said anxiously, "Then you know our house?"

I said, "That day you were wearing a red top with black leggings. When you got into the car, you unbuttoned your overcoat and said you had just come from exercise class. Shall I keep talking or have you heard enough?"

She said nervously, "Enough. What do you want to ask me?"

I said, "Someone who does this kind of shopping" pointing to her packages, "isn't struggling to come up with four or five thousand tomans. This ostentatious manner of yours doesn't jibe with extortion and coercion. What's the story?"

She said, "There's no extortion to it. No coercion either. That time I simply asked you for a loan and you willingly gave it. Just like this time, you weren't willing and you didn't give it."

I said, "Well, what came of the last loan?"

She opened up her purse and said, "I'll pay it back right now." And she took out five thousand tomans.

I said, "You said you didn't have any money!"

She answered, "And I don't have it now. This was emergency money."

I didn't take the money. She put it on the dashboard and said, "Take me home now and leave me alone."

I said, "Leave you alone? I've only just started with you. If you don't tell me the truth, I'll come knocking on all the doors in your neighborhood and ask all of your neighbors."

She said with fear in her voice, "You wanted your money, which I gave to you."

I said, "I didn't want my money and I didn't take it. But you can be sure I won't leave you alone until you tell me the whole truth."

She said, "What good will it do you to break my pride?"

I said, "I'm not trying to break your pride. I just want to know the truth."

She said, "What good will it do you to know the truth? What are all these secrets good for?"

I said, "I'll tell you later. After you tell me."

She said, "Ok, I'm really the maid at that house you saw. I go shopping one day a week for the lady of the house on the day she goes to class at the university. I wear her clothes. I take advantage of the stupidity and misdeeds of men. I pocket the fare by sweet-talking them out of collecting it. If the men fall into greed, which they normally do, I get a few thousand more out of it. And that's the whole story."

I said, "Take off your sunglasses."

Afraid, she said, "What for?"

I said, "I want to see your eyes."

Her hand was shaking as she removed her sunglasses, and facing me caused her to lower her gaze. Her eyes showed the desperation of a child whose sneakiness had been found out.

I said, "You were right to wear sunglasses, because you know well that a person's eyes give them away."

She put the sunglasses back on and said, "Let's go back now."

I asked, "Where did you learn all that fancy talk?"

She said, "I overheard the lady of the house talking with her students."

I asked, "How much longer did you think you could go on getting money like that?"

She said, "It could have gone on forever. Find a man who is truly a man, and then I'll tell you it will stop."

I said, "You mean if I was a real man, I wouldn't have given you a ride? Considering all those packages and all of your pleading?"

She said, "Giving a ride is one thing. But they think by giving me a loan, they are planting a seed that they will harvest later with the fake telephone number I give them."

I said, "Last time I gave you money, but I did not get your telephone number. How do you account for that?"

She said, "Stupidity. No offense to you."

I said, "Didn't you ever think you might run into these people again? Like today?"

She said, "Men can be tricked a thousand times over. I know this to be true – I've counted."

I asked, "You're not married?"

She said, "I am. He's a creep just like all men. He likes how I make all this money!"

I asked, "Aren't you afraid something bad might happen to you?"

She said, "Lots of bad things have happened to me. But someone who chooses to go down this road must be able to face what she encounters along the way."

I asked, "What do you expect to gain when you set yourself up to lose everything?"

She said, "Now are you going to starting preaching to me?"

I said, "Nevermind. Forget about it. We'll be at your door in a few minutes and that will be goodbye."

She said, "But you didn't answer my question. Why did you want to know my story?"

I answered, "Because I work with you. Or should I say, I work with your boss."

Terrified, she said, "You mean you teach Sociology?"

I said, "Something like that."

She looked pale in the face like she was about to faint. She gulped and asked weakly, "In the same university?"

I said, "No, a public university."

We arrived at Anahita alley and I said, "Very well, you can get out now. And take your money."

She took the money off the dashboard and put it in her purse. She opened the door and as she got out, she said, "I've always toyed with people, but this time I feel like I'm the one who has been toyed with."

I said, "In what way? You told the story yourself."

She got out and closed the door. Then she said, "It's like suddenly realizing that you're caught on hidden camera."

I said, "Then please hand me my cell phone you took."

She said, "Your cell phone?"

I said, "It's in your right pocket."

She took it out and handed it to me, "Sorry, old habits are hard to break."

I asked, "Didn't you think that since I know your address I would come to get it back from you?"

She said, "Actually, you don't know my address. Because that house that you thought I was going into was just a decoy. I knew you were watching me from your mirror."

"Then I'm the one who has been tricked, not you."

She said, "But I like you. I'll give you my phone number and you can call me if you want to."

I said, "I'm not interested. I got what I wanted."

She said, "And I take back what I said about being able to fool all men a thousand times over. Some men can't be fooled."

I said, "The problem is that you've never seen a real man before. None of the men you have seen were ever real men."

I Need a Leili

Leili and Majnoon are two lovers in ancient Iranian literature. Majnoon, a member of a noble family, falls in love with a gypsy girl named Leili, but the objections and rejections of the two families keeps them apart.

Majnoon literally means mad - and madness is the fate of this rational and honorable young man named Qeis Ameri who loses his sanity because of love.

This is of course the outer dimension of a story that has inner layers and dimensions which have made the story famous and immortal in the literary history of Iran.

We all laughed when Foad said, "I need a Leili."

And none of us took him seriously when he said, "I'm going crazy without a Leili in my life. I can't live without a Leili."

He said this so often that Saeed finally said, "No problem! I'll put a classified ad in the newspaper that reads, *'Wanted: a full-time Leili with a comfortable salary'*" and he went on to say, "I'll be damned if a flock of Leili's doesn't show up on your front doorstep tomorrow!"

And Yasser said, "All I have to do is drive around the block in my old clunker and an hour later I'll have five of them lined up for you, each one better than the next."

Shaking his head, Foad said, "Too bad that you are all donkeys; each one more of an idiot than the next!" We all laughed and began scoring each other's levels of idiocy.

Even back in those days when we would all call each other up and contrive a plan to show up at Foad's house without notice, we never imagined the issue would get this serious.

Mostafa had quite by accident seen Foad wandering around Tajrish Square with tousled hair and his whole appearance in a disheveled state asking anyone he passed, "Have you seen my Leili? Have you seen my Leili?"

And the people ranging from men and women and old and young would pass him by without giving any answer. Some would smile, some would pray for his mental health and still others would nod in mercy and sympathy as they passed him by.

Mostafa was telling us about how he had walked up to him and stood right there in front of him. In that delirious state, Foad asked Mostafa, "You ... have you seen my Leili?" and moments later when he realized it was Mostafa, he said in shock, "What are you doing here Mostafa?"

At first Mostafa wasn't sure what to say, but after a few moments he replied, "I'm looking for your Leili."

Foad took his hand and said, "Don't go looking for her, you'll never find her. If a true love, a soul mate, *a Leili* could be found, I would have found her by now after all this time searching."

Then he invited Mostafa back to his house for some tea, and confided in him, "Going on in life without a Leili is impossible for me."

Mostafa left Foad's house in shock. As soon as he got home, he called all of us to get over to Foad's house and think of something that could be done for him.

Foad was not an irrational man and had never suffered from any mental problems. Not only was he not irrational, he was a head above most people his age in understanding.

Even though he was only 27 or 28 years old, he had the wisdom and experience of a 40 year old man. Even though he had not yet married, he actually seemed more worldly than most of his married friends.

He studied hard in high school and graduated with honors. But all of a sudden after getting his diploma, he stopped pursuing his education and took refuge in poetry, singing and music.

He was a natural at poetry, had a good singing voice, and was talented in music. But he only did it for himself and didn't believe putting on performances. Not poetry, not music and not his singing. He would only oblige occasionally when we would all get together and ask him, or when he was in the mood to recite a poem or sing a song or play the sitar.

This happened much more than occasionally though, because Foad's house was a like a refuge for his married friends to get away from the hassle of daily life. That house was always our haven and shelter. His warmth and hospitality made us even more eager to go there.

It was about two years ago or perhaps more - two years and four months ago when Foad's mental condition became critical; I came to realize this sooner and better than the others because of my close friendship with him.

My diagnosis, which was later confirmed by psychologists, was depression. And the first symptom was that he had no desire to see anyone and this relatively cold treatment caused the guys to gradually quit coming to Foad's house.

But after that day in Tajrish Square, we just called Foad to make sure he was home, and we didn't tell him that we were all coming over. Each one of us was going to show up at Foad's house with fruit, sweets or something as if we were all showing up coincidentally - which of course, any fool could tell was planned.

Although his grooming was impeccable, you could see in Foad's face and the sorrow in his eyes that something was not right with him. This abnormality became even more apparent when we realized that he had no memory of his encounter with Mostafa in Tajrish Square and having tea with him afterwards.

I asked, "Foad, where have you been?"

As if responding to himself and not to me, he said, "In the valley of loneliness."

Mostafa said, "Foad won't get better until he marries. We should find him a good wife."

Foad shot a look at Mostafa and said, "What does loneliness have to do with having a wife or married life?"

And he turned to me and asked, "Take you, for example, Seyed, with so many wives and children, are you saying that you never feel lonely?"

I said, "What do you mean by *so many*? You make it seem like I ..."

Foad said, "I meant so many *years*. I mean being married with children for so many years. Loneliness has nothing to do with women and children and life. It's like saying that if Majnoon had simply married someone, he would have stuck to family life and would never have needed Leili. Right? But the concept of a true soul mate that I'm talking about - a love like Leili – can only be comprehended by those with a higher capacity for love."

Saeed pat Mostafa on the back and said, "I think Foad meant that you shouldn't talk too much."

We all laughed, but Foad said seriously, "Damn right." And of course, this confirmation was even funnier than his original admonition.

Saeed went on to say, "Of course, Foad! I think you're putting the cart before the horse. Majnoon didn't reach that intense desire for a soul mate before finding Leili, but it was after Leili came along when Majnoon began to suffer an from unbearable yearning for love; before that, Majnoon had been a rational and normal man by the name of Gheis Ameri."

Foad said, "You don't understand, Saeed."

And Mostafa readily interrupted his words, "You mean Saeed shouldn't talk so much?"

Foad said, "Well, yes, because Leili was not some obscure, hidden creature for Majnoon to have *discovered* her. Even before he saw her, Majnoon himself had a deep capacity for love, but he never found his match until Leili. How come other people who had met Leili didn't fall madly in love with her? A soul mate is a person's rare match on very deep levels."

To break the serious atmosphere, Yasser asked, "Well, what should we do now?"

Foad replied seriously, "Nothing. Get up and go on home."

And we all were surprised. Yasser was trying to be lighthearted and not show any hard feelings, he said, "I mean that if you need me to, I can play the role of Leili for awhile..."

Foad said, "No, thanks. I won't bother you."

Although his telling us to get up and go home was meant as a joke, we couldn't ignore the serious part of it.

That's why we all lingered a while and then little by little got up and left.

Yasser said, "Foad, my friend, we won't bother you anymore, but swear to God you'll take care of yourself. Finding or not finding a Leili is not worth ruining yourself."

Foad said, "If only ruination was the price to pay for finding a Leili. I am ready to offer my life for it."

There was an element of truth to Yasser's joke as he said, "Well, if this is the case, then you definitely need a psychiatrist."

Foad said, "And you need a veterinarian."

When we left Foad's house we were almost all unanimous that we needed to work out a solution for Foad's situation, but none of us could think of anything. We agreed to think about it on our own and then consult with each other and arrive at a common result.

However, I was restless. After saying goodbye to the guys, I went back to Foad's because I wanted to see what to do. Or what could be done?

Foad said, "I've tried everything but to no avail. I consulted domestic and foreign doctors, herbalists, chemists, psychiatrists and therapists, even mental health specialists, but none of them knew anything about this incurable pain. I tell them I can't work, and they tell me to exercise. I tell them I can't tolerate seeking anyone, they tell me to drink herbal teas. I say my spring of poetry has run out, they tell me to take a blood test. I tell them I don't want to live anymore, they give me pills. I say I need a Leili. They tell me to get married. I wonder sometimes what would happen if Leili, the symbol of this love, were not a woman; it would be better because then superficial people would not misinterpret this love."

I said, "It seems like no one but you has the power to do anything about this."

He said, "That is what I think. I have arrived at such a conclusion. But what to do and how to do it is still unclear."

To give hope I said, "Well this in itself is a ray of hope that one can find an answer."

He said, "To tell you the truth, I don't have much faith in your words. The fact that others can't do anything is obvious. But the idea that I can do something about it is mere wishful thinking. If something could be done, it would have been done by now."

I said, "How do you want to resolve this? It's really difficult what you're going through."

He said, "Difficult? More like impossible."

And with a choked voice he stressed, "Seyed! I am not living. I only count the moments until my death."

I tried to give solace to Foad that night in any language possible. But when I said good bye I realized that I had not been successful.

The next night, Foad was gone. He was neither at home nor anywhere else to be found. Not even the next night and day or the nights and days to follow.

The first one or two weeks we all considered it likely that he might have gone on a trip and would return soon. But there was still no word. And in the first and second months we searched for him wherever it occurred to us that he might be. But none of us found a trace of him.

And now that it is nearly two years since Foad has gone missing, we haven't given up and still search for him. But we all regret why when Foad said, "I need a Leili." None of us took the issue seriously even though we couldn't have done anything about it.

The Pink Negligee

It wasn't that the woman didn't understand the man's words; she just couldn't believe what he was saying. So she asked again, "*What* did you say I should do?"

The man replied, "This is the second time you're asking me this which makes it *three times* counting the first time I explained it to you!"

The woman said innocently, "Ok, let's say I'm obtuse; explain it to me once more."

The man said, "No, you're no dummy, that's why you're skeptical and surprised."

The woman said cynically, "You expect me to believe that you want to pay me this much money just to put something on for you? That's it?"

The man replied, "That's it!"

The woman said, "I have no problem with it, and I accept your proposition. But..."

The man said, "But what?"

She said, "But if I could know the reason behind it, I would be more comfortable with it."

He said, "Whether or not you are comfortable with it isn't important to me. What matters to me is that you do it."

She asked flirtingly, "Why me?"

And she expected to hear that it was because of her beauty and perfect figure. But the man didn't say these things.

He said, "Just because. Because you were the first person I asked."

She winced. He remembered the promise he had made to himself the night before and went over in his mind as he left the house that morning. *I will proposition the first woman who crosses my path to wear this negligee and free myself once and for all from this complex.*

A woman was at the corner selling fresh walnuts. She was holding several bags with a few walnuts in each. She was of medium height and looked to be about 25 or 26 years old. She had big, brown eyes framed by arching brows. She was neither fat nor thin. She had secured her chador by wrapping and tying the ends firmly around her waist, and over that she wore a fairly long, brown jacket buttoned all the way up.

The woman was standing right next to the man's car. He rolled down his window. She asked, "Do you want some walnuts?"

He said, "All of them, perhaps."

And the light turned green.

He said, "Meet me on the other side of the intersection."

After he passed through the intersection, he gradually pulled over and from his rear view mirror he could see the woman running up to his car.

When he stopped, she appeared at his car window again. She asked, "Do you really want to buy all of them?"

And he let out a laugh. "Ok tell me, how much per bag?"

She answered, "Five hundred each. But if you're buying them all, I'll charge only 450 each."

He said, "I'll pay for them all, but you keep your walnuts. But will you do something for me in exchange?"

She said, "I'm not into any hanky-panky. Let me set that straight right now."

He said, "Who is nowadays? Nobody's into hanky-panky nowadays!"

She said, "What do you want me to do?"

He said, "Not much. I just want you to put this on for me, and let me see it on you. That's all."

She answered hesitatingly, "Fine."

He said, "Get in."

She blurted, "Get in?"

He said sarcastically, "No, put it on right here in the intersection!"

They both smiled. She walked around to the passenger side of the car and opened the door and sat down beside him. She put the bags of walnuts down on the floor of the car beside her legs and said, "I've got to be back here by noon. My sister will be picking me up."

The man accelerated and said, "Don't worry. I'll have you back in one hour."

The woman looked at the dashboard and the seats and said, "What a beautiful car! Lucky for your wife who sits in this seat!"

With a forced smile he said, "For now it's you who is sitting in it."

She was taken aback as she said, "I wouldn't want to disrupt your life."

He smiled a bitter smile and said, "No worries. You've still got some growing to do."

She said, "What do you mean by that?"

He said, "Nevermind."

She said, "Well, I trusted you that I got into your car."

With her same tone he replied, "And I trusted you that I let you get in."

He stopped in front of the house and said, "Ok, we're here."

Before getting out, she said anxiously, "You never said why you wanted to see the dress on me?"

As he put the windows up, he said, "What difference does it make to you?"

She said, "No difference. I just liked to know."

He opened the door to the building with his key and said to her, "Please, after you."

She looked around carefully before stepping in. "I hope it won't be bad for you if the neighbors see me going inside."

He closed the door and said, "Don't worry about it. People wouldn't think anything wrong with this combination."

She asked, "What do you mean by this *combination*?"

He said indifferently, "I mean what you see."

This obviously insulted her and she protested, "Are you talking about my appearance?"

He directed her into the living room, and wanting to mollify her he said, "I didn't mean anything by it. You're asking futile questions."

She stood next to the couch wondering what to do. "What would you like me to do?"

He said, "Have a seat and I'll bring you some tea."

She sat down on the couch and said candidly, "When I asked you *'why me'* I was hoping to hear a white lie."

Even though he knew what she meant, he asked, "A lie? What kind of lie?"

She said, "I don't know, something. The kind of things girls like to hear."

He sat down on the couch next to her. "I understand. I also like to hear these things, but nobody has ever said them to me, so I'm not used to saying them or hearing them."

She said, "I imagine the dress you want me to put on is a dress you wanted to see on your wife, but she won't wear it for you, right?"

He was taken aback. It was the only thing he didn't expect to hear. "How do you know that?"

With an artificial air, she said, "Well, we women understand things that men don't - and when they see that we do, it surprises them."

He started opening up to her because he felt she disarmed him, "It's not just this dress. All the nightgowns I have ever bought for her are stuffed in her closet. When she comes home from work, she puts on drab houseclothes and does housework. And then she comes to bed in those same clothes."

Tears welled up in her eyes. "But my life has been the opposite. I did whatever a female could do to attract him back to our life, but he wouldn't turn away from his opium smoking. He finally ended up in jail, and I ended up selling goods on the streets."

He asked, "Did you divorce him?"

She said, "Honestly, no. Because I still love him - even though he ruined my life." And she started to cry.

He got up and took an opened present from the telephone table and put it in front of her. It was a pink chiffon nightgown with pink lace ties. She opened it and held it out in front of her. "It's beautiful."

He said, "It's yours. You don't have to put it on. Take it with you."

She was surprised, "Why have you changed your mind?"

He said, "I just did. Wear it for yourself. I wanted to see it on her, but now it doesn't matter to me anymore."

He got up and went into the bedroom and came back with three opened bottles of perfume and placed them in front of her. "And these are for you too. These won't be used in this house."

She was delighted, "But why?"

He said, "Let's go or you'll be late."

She said, "We're leaving?"

He said, "Yes, I'm going to be late too."

She picked up all her gifts and got up to leave.

They were silent the whole way back. When she was getting out of the car, she asked, "Are you crazy?"

He answered, "I wasn't before, but I am now."

Breaking the News

More troubling than the death itself of Haj Davood, was how to break it to his son, which suddenly turned into a problem for us.
Anyone hearing the news of Haj Davood's sudden death, would say before anything else, "Oh, Poor Mamal! He's coming home to see his father after being in America for twenty years!"
Haj Davood was easily in his sixties, but he wasn't about to die. He was strong and on his feet. He loved to exercise, hike and take long walks; of course, he also liked to smoke a lot.
Anyhow, news of his death was so unexpected that it plunged everybody into amazement and disbelief.
They first announced it as a heart attack, to get people ready.

Hamid phoned me saying that Haj Davood was having heart trouble and that they had taken him to the Critical Care Unit. He asked if we could all get together and see what could be done.

I said, "He's in CCU – there's no need to get together. All we need to do is visit him. Poor Mamal, he hasn't seen his father in twenty years and now he has to visit him in the CCU. Now, which hospital is it? Hopefully, he's out of danger."

Choked up with tears, Hamid said, "No, to tell you the truth, no, he's not."

I said, "What do you mean?"

He burst into tears and said, "I mean there's no hope."

And the phone cut off, either purposefully or accidentally. And after a few more calls it became clear that Haj Davood had crashed on the Caspian Highway and died instantly. He had been driving alone. As always when he needed to escape the hustle and bustle of Tehran, he would resort to the mountains and woods in the north for peace and solace.

As Hamid suggested, the first thing to do as his closest friends was to get together and see what should be done.

None of us had any news about his wife nor did we know how to inform her. We didn't even know if it was necessary.

Haj Davood and his wife had separated twenty years before and sent Mamal to the US. Each of them had separate lives and Haj Davood usually did not like to talk about his ex-wife and her life.

Therefore, informing her did not seem to be urgent. We, his close buddies, needed to get together and make all of the funeral arrangements, the most important of which was breaking the news to Mamal, who would be arriving in Tehran two days later after a twenty-year absence, and rather than hearing the warm voice of his father, would be hearing the news of his death.

The arrangements took place smoothly. With the contacts Jalal had at the morgue and the Behesht-e-Zahra Cemetery, the funeral ceremonies were accomplished quickly and prestigiously on the morning of the next day after his death. That afternoon we gathered at the home of the late Haj Davood primarily to plan how to break the news to Mamal, and secondly to plan the funeral wake.

Jalal believed, "Right after his arrival, we should just come right out with it plainly and get it over with. This will make it easier on both Mamal and everybody else."

Almost all were opposed to this view and argued, "This way is the worst possible way to do it."

Even Javad said sarcastically, "How about just taking him directly from the airport to the Behesht-e-Zahra Cemetery and when he asks 'where are you taking me?' we'll say 'to your father's grave!' What you're suggesting is pretty much the same thing!"

Hamid said, "I think we should tell him gradually."

Mocking him, Javad chimed in, "I mean, first we should say 'your father is somewhat dead' and then little by little ..."

Hamid said, "No, dummy! I mean, first we should say he had a heart attack and is in the hospital and then ..."

Teasing him, Javad interjected, "And perhaps we will show him another patient in the hospital and tell him that his father's face totally changed after the heart attack."

There was a dish of dates on the table which was customary on these occasions. People would take one as they said a silent prayer for the deceased.

Saeed said, "I have a better idea!" as he grabbed a fistful of the dates and was about to pop them into his mouth when Javad grabbed his hand and said, "Hold on there! What are you doing? A whole busload of people hasn't crashed! One man has died!"

Saeed reluctantly put the extra dates back in the dish and said, "Now, are you going to let me talk or not?"

Javad replied, "Talk as much as you want! Words are unlimited. It is dates that are limited as far as quantity is concerned! Not only that, but may God have mercy on you as I hear you're a diabetic as well?"

Saeed said, "Mamal hasn't set out yet. Has he?"

Everyone nodded that he hadn't.

Saeed went on to say, "Then we'll send out a fax or an email on behalf of Haj Davood for him to postpone his visit. We'll come up with a good excuse. That way we can buy some time so as to think out a solution to this problem."

Javad said, "I think this is the worst thing you could do because first of all, there *is* no solution to this problem; it would only put it on the back burner. Secondly, in the meantime, he might find out about it anyway, and what we were trying to avoid happening would happen anyway."

Mohsen said, "What if we told him his dad went on a trip?"

Javad burst into laughter.

Mohsen asked angrily, "Why are you laughing?"

Javad said, "You think Mamal will believe it with all the letters, phone calls and previous arrangements he made with Haj Davood to see him? Of course, we can say that he's gone on an eternal trip and hope that he gets our drift!"

This time, Saeed said cautiously, "I've got one more idea, and I'll tell you only if Javad promises not to laugh."

Javad placed his hand over his mouth and said, "Zipped! I promise not to say a word. Tell us!"

Saeed said, "Mamal has not seen his father for the past 20 years. Isn't that right?"

Again, everybody nodded.

Saeed went on to say, "What if one of us who resembles him more pretends to be his father? How about Hamid - who looks a lot like Haj Davood? (not now, of course!) Mamal won't be here forever. Hamid could play the role of Haj Davood for just a short while and then everything will be fine."

Javad said, "Look, Saeed! It is not my fault. Your plan is essentially absurd."

Hamid said, "If in this scenario Haj Davood and his wife get back together, then I'm ready to play this role."

Saeed said indignantly, "You're being ridiculous! Otherwise, what's wrong with this plan?"

Javad said, "It's true that they haven't seen each other in years, but they've surely sent photos and videos. And Mamal was never dull that you take him for an idiot. He's sharp. He'll easily figure it out. Not only that, it's not just about what his father *looks like*. What about all their history together which we know nothing about? This Haj Hamid of ours with his rich intelligence that he treasures will ruin everything in the first three or four minutes ... Well, ... Is that enough or shall I continue?"

Saeed said in protest against Javad, "You who find fault with everybody else's suggestions, do you have anything better in mind?"

Javad said with an air self-assurance, "Of course, I do. Just entrust the whole issue to me and watch how I resolve it."

They all asked curiously, "Oh, really? How? What's your solution?"

Javad said matter-of-factly, "We'll all go to the airport together to welcome Mamal and tell him that his father is at home and that he sprained his ankle and couldn't come. Then on the way home, I'll break the news to him myself in my own special way."

Everybody said "Bravo" and unanimously confirmed this plan.

ርዊ፩

We were all sitting in the arrivals hall waiting for Mamal's plane to land. Recognizing him wasn't hard because we had all seen the latest photographs that he had sent displayed in Haj Davood's house. As a rule, he should have known us because Haj Davood had sent Mamal all the pictures of us in the mountains, on trips, and at friends' parties, and he told us that he had spoken about each of us to Mamal.

Despite the fact that we all had prepared ourselves in advance for his return, as soon as we saw his face on the big screen in the arrival hall, we all fell apart. We were all choked up and some of us couldn't hold back the tears. Haj Davood's absence was just now sinking in.

Javad was a little more resilient and reserved than the rest of us. "What is the *matter* with you all?" he snapped, "Don't you know you're supposed to *control* yourselves? This way you'll spoil everything!"

We all dropped our heads in embarrassment and tried to pull ourselves together as we sniffled and dried our tears, and forced ourselves to smile.

It took what seemed a life time, not half an hour, for Mamal to go through customs and enter the arrival hall. We all gathered ourselves around with seemingly happy and smiling faces as we moved towards Mamal to welcome him. Fortunately, he recognized us from afar and walked over to us.

We were still a few steps away from each other, when Javad separated from the group. He walked one or two steps forward, opened his arms to hug Mamal and began weeping, not crying in a normal calm way, but sobbing, wailing and moaning. Amid all this, he suddenly yelled, "Mamal, your father died!"

As they embraced with Javad's back to us, we witnessed both astonishment and bewilderment in Mamal's face, who was looking at us with eyes agog and mouth wide open. Perhaps he was looking at our shock at Javad's unexpected behavior.

At first we thought that Mamal's shock was because he didn't know what had happened. But by his reaction, we realized that fortunately he understood everything at Javad's very first sentence. Most of all, he understood our trepidation about how to relay this terrible news to him and the likely consequences, which as it turned out, was all in vain.

He acted like one who had just missed the first morning bus, shook his head with regret and said, "Oh man! ... What a pity! ... I've just brought him a new pair of hiking boots!"

The Spitting Image

A man asked a woman who nurtured a strong sense of being beautiful, "Excuse me! You're not Sharon Stone, are you?"

The woman said vainly, "No, but..."

And before she could speak, the man said, "Well, I thought because ..."

The woman interrupted him, "Yes, many say the resemblance is uncanny. Is it not?"

The man said resolutely, "No, it isn't. They're all wrong because Sharon Stone is a beautiful woman, but unfortunately you're not beautiful at all. That's why I didn't think you were Sharon Stone."

When she realized that she had been tricked, she screeched indignantly, "You villain! How could you talk to a lady like that? Don't you have a sister or a mother?"

The man said calmly, "Sure I do, but neither of them brag about looking like Sharon Stone."

Still angry, the woman said, "So what's wrong with it?"

The man said, "Since you think you look like Sharon Stone, I just wanted to disillusion you."

The woman got angry again, "Go disillusion your mother!"

The man went on to explain calmly, "I told you my mother has no such illusion about herself, but since you do ..."

The woman screamed, "It's none of your damn business what assumption I have of myself!" and she picked up her bag as if she were about to hit him with it.

The man dodged and tried to continue on his way.
But the woman didn't stop. Three and four people gathered around hoping to see a good fight.

One told the man, "Where are you going? Wait and see what she wants."

The other one said, "This is very unbecoming of a man of such high caliber like you!" pointing to the man's suit.

The third one said, "This young lady is like your daughter. It's just not decent."

The woman shouted at the man who kept aloof of her, "You just say whatever comes out of your mouth and then drop your head like a cow and walk away?"

Someone asked, "What's wrong madam? Is this man harassing you?"

The woman, who kept running after the man with the three or four other people following behind her said, "He has done worse than harass me, that filthy man!"

ಬಂಐ

Down at the police station before the officer on duty had the chance to ask any questions, the woman said, "Captain! I would like to file a complaint against this man for insulting me!"

The officer on duty turned his head to the man who was neatly fixing his gray hair and said, "Is that right?"

The man said, "All I told her is that she didn't look like Sharon Stone. If this remark is an insult, well then I must have insulted her."

The officer on duty was staring open-mouthed at the woman. She drew back her head scarf to the extent that two locks of hair framed her face like parentheses.

The officer could not take his eyes off of her.

The woman said, "What is it to him who I look like?"

The officer told the man, "It is none of your business who she looks like."

The man said, "Are you an echo?"

The officer said, "What do you mean by echo?"

The man said, "I mean an amplifier that repeats the sound."

The officer said, "Answer my question!"

The man said, "I am living in this society. How can I be indifferent to the problems around me? I saw an old woman yesterday imagining herself to be Sophia Loren. It took a long time for me to make her understand that this was not true. I don't think she finally accepted it. Yesterday, I was at Station 13 with Captain Manochehri on a similar complaint."

The officer on duty was sitting upright, confidently pulled his pen from his pocket and arranged the paperwork in front of him.

He said, "So, disturbing the ladies is your everyday business, is that right?"

The man said, "No. Not every day. Just whenever I get the chance. Twice a day - once in a while. Of course, it is not just the ladies that I harass; I have a similar problem with men as well. Some people think they are Marlon Brando; some others imagine being

Arnold Schwarzenegger and they don't only imagine themselves as actors ..."

The woman took out a small mirror from her bag and wiped traces of mascara from under her eyes with facial tissue and as she put the mirror back into her bag she said, "A professional harasser! How great that you were caught!"

The officer on duty said, "Of course, with the wisdom of the law enforcement and the tireless, vigilant and watchful eye of the police force."

The woman said in surprise, "Yes?"

The officer on duty said, "Well, we think of you as one of our own."

The woman said vainly, "How do you mean?! I barely know you but you act like a close friend!"

The officer on duty ignored her snide remark and shouted, "Ashtiani! Fetch us some tea!"

A soldier opened the door and kept a stiff step, "Yes Captain. And he left the room."

The man said, "See captain! I am not a professional harasser. I was not running away to have been caught. Whenever I have given reprimands, I have paid the cost. I have also been taken in to the police station. I am not indebted to anybody."

The office on duty said bitterly, "Save your arguments for the court."

And he put a piece of paper in front of the man and said, "Write down your complaint."

The man quickly wrote down his statement and handed back the piece of paper. The officer on duty gave the piece of paper to the woman and said, "Now you also write down your complaint."

By the time Ashtiani knocked at the door, entered by permission, saluted and placed the cups of tea on the table, the woman had finished writing down her statement and handed the sheet of paper back to the officer on duty.

After a brief review, the officer confirmed with the woman, "This is your home number?

The woman said, "Yes, it is my home number."

The officer said, "If possible please also write down your mobile number as well. It might be necessary."

The woman was about to take back the sheet of paper when the officer gave her instead, a small piece of paper and said, "You can just write it on this."

The man said, "Would you like me to give you my mobile number as well?"

The officer paused and said, "Sure, go ahead, no problem."

The man said, "I don't have a mobile phone."

The officer on duty grit his teeth, "Then why are you asking?"

The man said, "I wanted to see if it is all right that I don't have a mobile phone? I don't know the laws, that is why ..."

The officer on duty said, "No, it's ok that you don't have a mobile phone."

And he asked the woman, "What should I write is the reason for your complaint?"

And the man replied instead, "Write that I accused her of not looking like Sharon Stone."

And he turned to the woman, "If I have insulted you in any other way, please say what it was."

The woman said, "He's still harassing me."

The man said, "But you called me villain, filthy, cow and other things which I will raise in my complaint later."

The woman was taken aback and said, "Well, you made me angry."

And she asked the officer on duty, "What happens now?"

The officer on duty said, "Once the case is documented, I will forward it to the court where the judge will issue the verdict."

The man asked, "Will the judge issue a ruling on her assumption that she looks like Sharon Stone or not?" And he went on to say, "The judge has a very difficult job, you know, if he really wants to investigate properly."

The officer on duty replied, "No, he will issue a verdict regarding your alleged harassment of the lady."

And he looked at his watch and said, "Well, the office is now closing. You will stay here tonight and go to court for your hearing tomorrow."

The man told the woman, "Now that look more closely, you don't look very different from Sharon Stone."

The woman said, "Do you really think so?"

The man said, "Really, if this similarity did not exist why would I mention Sharon Stone out of so many actresses?"

The woman said, "Many people have said so. I wish I could meet Sharon Stone and know her opinion."

The man said, "She would definitely admit this similarity."

The woman told the officer on duty, "I want to cancel my complaint. I don't really have the patience to go to court and go through this process. Tear up the complaint and throw it out."

The officer on duty said, "I can't. The law has to be carried out."

The woman asked in amazement, "But I'm withdrawing my complaint ..."

The officer on duty said, "True, but what about the law?"

The man said, "The law has her mobile number."

The officer on duty feigned not to have heard and told the woman it would be difficult but that he would somehow settle it.

The man stood up to leave. He turned to the officer on duty and said, "There has been a question lingering in my mind since I arrived at the police station. May I ask?"

While tearing up the papers, the officer on duty said, "Go ahead."

The man said, "Don't you think you resemble Sherlock Holmes?"

Afsaneh

Samira put some canned fruit into the refrigerator by my bed and said, "How are you doing?"

I said, "So kind of you to ask."

With a more or less angry look, she glared at me and said, "Sarcasm again?"

I said, "*'So kind of you to ask'* is a common expression. Where is there sarcasm in that?"

She slammed the refrigerator door in a way that made the vase of daffodils on top of it rock from side to side, freeing her hands to wave in the air and raising her voice a little, "When I ask how you are, you can simply reply *'I'm better'* or *'I'm not better'* but when you answer *'So kind of you to ask'* it implies you're blaming it all on me and I..."

I sat up in the bed and said, "Listen here, madam! This place is not our house, it's the CCU of a hospital. Whoever hasn't yet figured out the reason for my heart attack, will do so with this scene you're making. Let's have a ceasefire until we figure things out.

She said, "What's there to figure out?"

I said, "Life and death."

She answered with that same fury, "That's not happening. You'll be fine in a few days."

I said, "I'm sorry for you."

The nurse tapped on the door and came in with a tray of medicines. There was a syringe, a small cup with several colorful pills in it, and an ampoule. She said hello to us and placed the tray on the rolling table in front of me.

Samira said to the nurse, "We've put you to a lot of trouble."

The nurse smiled sweetly and said, "Incidentally, not at all."

And my mind went to the existential philosophy of "incidentally" when Samira asked, "Do we know when he might be released?"

The nurse handed me a cup of water and the pills and said, "In the next few days. Thank God he's getting much better."

Samira turned to me and self-righteously said, "See?"

The nurse was surprised at Samira's tone of voice and looked at both of us. I said indifferently to Samira, "Go ahead and continue with making a scene. The conditions are favorable."

Samira bit her lip and the nurse blurted, "A scene?"

I said, "Yes, I have decided to get myself a companion to spend my spare time with, and she is against it."

Samira looked at me dumbstruck at this unexpected comment and said innocently, "When have I ever objected to this?"

I said, "So you're ok with it?"

She said, "No, because you already have so many companions."

I said, "I wasn't talking about that kind of friend. I was talking about a different kind friend."

She said encouragingly, "I'm happy you finally agree - because none of your friends are the right kind of people!"

I said, "I don't mean kind, I mean gender."

She furled her eyebrows and her eyes grew small as she said, "What do you mean?"

I said, "I mean that all my other companions were men. This one might be a little different."

She asked in disbelief, "You mean this one might be a woman?"

I muttered under my breath, "Or maybe a young woman."

The nurse pushed aside the bedsheet, grit her teeth and pushed the shot in firmly.

Samira forced an artificial smile at the nurse and said, "See? He even jokes from a hospital bed!"

The nurse smiled, but I wasn't smiling when I said, "See? She won't take even an important issue like this, seriously!"

And I turned to Samira and said, "Madam! This time it might be a little more serious than ever before."

Samira shrugged and said, "I've always said, I have nothing to worry about. You're not capable of doing it."

I said, "Well, if I *am* capable, it's kind of hard to show it from a hospital bed."

She challenged, "An incapable person is incapable wherever he is. It has nothing to do with being in the hospital."

I said, "Very well. Then if I go after proving my capability, you shouldn't get too upset."

Like always, she answered indignantly, "What would I get upset for? A fleabite?"

I said, "Even if I've already made my choice?"

She sighed and said, "Of course, I'd like to see her."

I said, "I'm certain you've seen her. I wouldn't choose someone you've never seen. I'm not that impudent."

The nurse said, "Are you doing ok, Mr. Azizi?"

I said teasingly, "Yes, I am, but why do you ask me how I am without even so much as an introduction?" She took the thermometer from above my bed and shook it, then brought it up to my mouth. She said, "I think you may have a fever. Your symptoms indicate that." She put the thermometer in my mouth. "Incidentally, the doctor recommends that you keep talk to a minimum."

Samira said in disbelief, "It's impossible for you to have done such a thing."

I replied indifferently, "It's not that impossible."

She asked with a childlike curiosity, "What's her name? Tell me her name."

I said, "Her name is not important. Let's pretend it's Afsaneh."

The nurse was leaving the room when I called after her, "Afsaneh?"

She turned around and clumsily looked at us both. Samira grabbed the side of the bed to keep herself from falling down.

Presently, Samira is in the CCU of that same hospital, sleeping on that very bed and Afsaneh and I spare nothing in our efforts to get her well.

When I'm at work, Afsaneh takes care of her and when Afsaneh has her shift, I get myself over to the hospital to look after her. And when we are both over at the hotel near the hospital, the other nurses perform our responsibilities to the best of their abilities.

About the Author

Renowned author Seyed Mehdi Shojaee was born in 1960 in Tehran. He is famous for his outstanding books on spiritual themes. After obtaining his high school diploma in mathematics, Shojaee entered the Dramatic Arts Faculty where he was conferred a Bachelor's Degree in Dramatic Literature. Simultaneously, he studied Political Science at Tehran University's Faculty of Law and Political Science, but left his studies unfinished to pursue a career in writing. At the age of 20, his early works were published as serial stories in newspapers. For the next eight years, he worked as Cultural Editor of the Persian daily Jomhouri-e Eslami Newspaper and for another eight years subsequent to that as Editor-in-Chief at the monthly Sahifeh.

Seyed Mehdi Shojaee has authored a number of plays and scripts. He has translated and written over 100 books for children and young adults. During 1986-1996, he was a juror for the Fajr International Film Festival, the Esfahan International Festival of Film and Video for Children and Young Adults, the Fajr International Theatre Festival and the National Press Festival. He is an Iranian cinema and theatre critic. He was on the Board of Directors of the Institute for the Intellectual Development of Children and Young Adults for some years.

He has written a play script on the life of the Martyr Mostafa Chamran for a TV series as well as a play script about Joseph for the Islamic Republic of Iran Broadcasting. Among other scripts authored by Seyed Mehdi Shojaee are "Badouk", "Father" (directed by Majid Majidi) and "Bat's Eye." Some of his religious works include "Sun in Veil", "Father, Love and Son," "The Berthed Ship," "Two Pigeons," and "Two Windows." He is the founder of Neyestan Book Publishing House which has been a reputable Iranian publisher of the works of contemporary writers and poets since 1987.

About the Translator

Caroline Croskery is a lifelong American student of Iranian Studies, highly proficient in the Persian language, and dearly devoted to the Persian culture. She was born in the United States and moved to Iran at the age of twenty-one. She holds a Bachelor's Degree from the University of California at Los Angeles in Iranian Studies where she graduated Cum Laude. For many years, she has been active in three fields of specialization: Language Teaching, Translation and Interpretation and Voiceover Acting.

During her thirteen years living in Iran, she taught English and also translated and dubbed Iranian feature films into English. After returning to live in the United States, she began a ten year career as a court interpreter and translator of books from Persian into English. She is an accomplished voiceover talent, and currently continues her voiceover career in both English and Persian.

Other titles translated and narrated by Caroline Croskery are:

Languor of the Morn, by Fattaneh Haj Seyed Javadi

We Are All Sunflowers, by Erfan Nazarahari

Democracy or Democrazy, by Seyed Mehdi Shojaee

In the Twinkling of an Eye, by Seyed Mehdi Shojaee

The Water Urn, by Houshang Moradi Kermani

A Sweet Jam, by Houshang Moradi Kermani

The Little Goldfish, with Audio CD Narration by Katayoun Riahi

Mullah Nasreddin, illustrated by Alireza Golduzian

The Paper Boat, written and illustrated by Anahita Taymourian

The Circus Outside the Window, written and illustrated by Anahita Taymourian

Sleep Full of Sheep, written and illustrated by Pejman Rahimizadeh

Stillness in a Storm, Collection of Poetry in Persian and English by Saeid Ramezani (also available on Aubible)

Made in the USA
Middletown, DE
17 August 2019